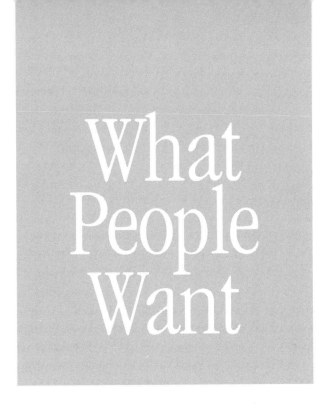

What
People
Want

A Manager's Guide to
Building Relationships That Work

Terry R. Bacon

Davies-Black Publishing
Mountain View, California

Published by Davies-Black Publishing, a division of CPP, Inc., 1055 Joaquin Road, 2nd Floor, Mountain View, CA 94043; 800-624-1765.

Special discounts on bulk quantities of Davies-Black books are available to corporations, professional associations, and other organizations. For details, contact the Director of Marketing and Sales at Davies-Black Publishing: 650-691-9123; fax 650-623-9271.

Visit the Davies-Black Publishing Web site at www.daviesblack.com.

10 09 08 07 06   10 9 8 7 6 5 4 3 2 1

Printed in the United States of America

Library of Congress Cataloging-in-Publication Data
Bacon, Terry R.
  What people want : a manager's guide to building relationships that work / Terry Bacon.—1st ed.
    p. cm.
  Includes bibliographical references and index.
  ISBN-13: 978-0-89106-216-5 (hardcover)
  ISBN-10: 0-89106-216-5 (hardcover)
  1. Communication in personnel management. 2. Interpersonal relations.
    I. Title.
  HF5549.5.C6B235 2006
  658.3'145—dc22
                                                                              2006029719
FIRST EDITION
First printing 2006

Contents

Preface

In one way or another, I have been leading and managing people for the past thirty-five years. For the last sixteen of those years, I have been the president of Lore International Institute, a firm that provides executive assessment, coaching, and education throughout the world. During my years as an educator and coach, I have been privileged to work with thousands of managers who have, for the most part, done their best to lead others and manage their operations effectively. They have taught me that management is at once the most challenging of vocations and the most rewarding, and that the principal challenge for most of them is not managing technology, systems, operations, finances, or other resources but managing people.

As a student of psychology and an observer of people at their best and less than best, I am convinced that few forces in nature are as complex and sometimes difficult to fathom as the typical human being. We are an astonishing blend of chemical and electrical impulses, histories, drives, conflicts, intentions, affinities, biases, hopes, joys, frustrations, and fears—and when you put us together in teams or organizations that interact with a complex environment over time, the dazzling array of behaviors, attitudes, and relationships is nothing short of stunning. Our brains have evolved from a primitive reptilian core to three pounds of an extraordinarily rich effusion of neurons that permit higher-level cognition as well as consciousness, the capacity for creativity and art, and a genius for discerning the truths of nature. Yet we have difficulty mastering our emotions and often act irrationally, particularly toward one another.

In the seven decades or so that most of us have on this earth, we struggle to make meaning in our lives, and a fundamental component of that meaning is our work. What we do and how well we do it is a source of safety and security. More than that, however, it is a wellspring of pride, a primary basis for self-esteem, and one of the foundations of identity. Consequently, most people take work very seriously, and most do their work in organizations where some people organize the work, deploy the people to do the work, and oversee the organization's systems, processes, and outcomes. I wrote this book for them, for the millions of people in the world of work who have those management roles.

I wrote it partly because I wanted to share some of what I've learned about managing people but also because it was a helpful way to explore my own experiences as a manager. It helps to step back now and then and reflect on what you've done well and what you might have done better. I've been blessed in my decades as a teacher and coach to witness both some profoundly effective acts of management and leadership and some stupendously awful ones as well. As I've observed the effective ones, I've marveled at how gracefully those managers behaved—how kind, how considerate, how bold, and often how insightful and creative. And as I've witnessed the ineffective ones, I've wondered how otherwise bright people could have reacted with such unprofessional behavior. Nonetheless, I'm convinced that most managers are doing their best or trying to. By and large, they act with good intentions but often don't realize the negative impact their behavior is having or what price they are paying in terms of lost trust, credibility, and employee goodwill.

Through the years, I have coached many managers who needed help building better relationships with their employees. They realized that management and leadership are mostly about working with and guiding other people, and if they weren't naturally talented at building great relationships with the people they managed, they usually weren't sure what to do differently. This book is for them. In it, I am offering hundreds of suggestions for building trust, creating a respectful environment, being sensitive to others, setting the right tone, and developing the kinds of employee relationships that result in lower turnover, higher productivity, and much greater employee satisfaction—all of which are keys to running efficient and profitable enterprises.

Acknowledgments

I could not have written a book like this without the help of many other people. First, I would like to acknowledge and thank the thousands of executives and professionals I have worked with as an educator, coach, counselor, or consultant. Whatever I've given them pales beside what they have given me. You can't teach others without simultaneously having them teaching you.

I would also like to thank the people who read the manuscript and offered valuable insights, suggestions, and corrections. They include Phyllis Lea, Martin Moller, Maryann Billington, and Terryl Leroux, who are colleagues at Lore International Institute. Phyllis, an extraordinary people person, was especially helpful in brainstorming chapter content. Like me, she is an imperfect veteran at human relations (actually, we all are), but she has great ideas and was a valuable thought partner on this project. Likewise, Martin, Maryann, and Terryl had a number of useful suggestions and observations. I am particularly indebted to Martin for his permission to talk about his theater project.

I want to give special thanks to Donna Stewart, my research associate at Lore. She was invaluable in every phase of this project, from the research on relationship needs to editing and proofing the final manuscript. I also want to thank Bruce Spining, who helped considerably in the data gathering, and Joey Maceyak, who programmed the data analysis and gave me the means to view, understand, and interpret the results. Finally, many thanks to Bill Doherty, whose psychometric insights were instrumental in understanding which research results were significant.

Thanks also to Tom Fuhrmark and Sheri Ligtenberg for their capable assistance. Tom created the visuals for the book, and Sheri proofread it. They both made me look better. Thanks to Karen McKibbin, who told some wonderful stories about her grandmother, Dorothy McKibbin; Marian Fry, who offered many powerful observations about people; and especially Virginia Lashbrooke, a friend and psychologist who read the manuscript closely and, over a series of lunches, was profoundly helpful to me. Her keen insights about people, particularly those in management positions, were instrumental in many of the chapters of this book. Thanks, Ginny.

Many thanks as well to a wonderful friend and thought partner, Connie Kallback, my editor at Davies-Black. In writing this book and my previous Davies-Black book, *Adaptive Coaching,* I have been blessed to have an editor of uncommon humanity as well as perceptiveness.

I also want to thank family and friends: Jennifer, Tom, Faith, and Tommy Neary; Tom, Bryn, Mira, and Sten Joyner; Shalley Parmenter; Darrin, Andrea, and Elena Grace Parmenter; Mildred and Lou Prevosti; Christopher and Chris Ann Pietig; Michael and Carlin Jo Kammerer; Kimberly and Chuck Regan; my many nieces, nephews, great-nieces and great-nephews; John Kenneth Christian; Scotty Nix; and others too numerous to name, who are the notes in the songs I sing. Without their love and friendship, nothing is possible.

Finally, I want to thank Debra Parmenter, who has done more for this book and for my soul than she realizes. She is one of those people whose humanity is etched in every feature and whose character is reflected in the lives of every person she has touched through her giving spirit and community service. If the night sky had a star for everything she has done for me, there would be no darkness. My love and thanks to this very special woman.

About the Author

Terry R. Bacon, PhD, is founder and chairman of Lore International Institute, a global executive development firm specializing in executive assessment, education, coaching, and organizational development consulting. In the past three decades, he has taught, consulted with, and coached thousands of executives in Fortune 500 companies. His clients have included AT&T, American Express, General Electric, Ford, General Motors, General Dynamics, McDonald Douglas, Boeing, Siemens, Hewlett-Packard, Centex, Bank of America, Chase Bank, Nike, Raytheon, Westinghouse, Avaya, Fluor, KBR, and Cargill. Bacon is a prolific author and popular speaker. His most recent books are *Winning Behavior, The Behavioral Advantage, Adaptive Coaching, Selling to Major Accounts,* and *Powerful Proposals.* He lives in Durango, Colorado.

Introduction

If you manage or lead other people, your success and the success of your group or organization depend to a great extent on your ability to build effective relationships with the people you manage. Several years ago I was asked to coach John, a manager who was a good administrator but ineffective at managing people. In his company's latest employee survey and 360-degree feedback, he was ranked among the lowest in his peer group in nearly all areas related to the people side of management. Furthermore, his group was highest in employee turnover and lowest in retention of high potentials. As I got to know John, I found him to be competent and well organized, with a fine eye for detail and a deep knowledge of the business. He seemed personable and friendly during our first meeting, but as I got to know him I found that his engagement with people was short-lived. He could appear charming and caring for moments, but underneath he was an efficiency engine that never stopped running, and when the perceived need to engage with people passed, he reverted quickly to the taskmaster he really was.

Still, John recognized that management had another side that wasn't all about planning, organizing, and driving execution. He was aware that the people working for him respected him but did not like him. He knew they thought he was cold and insensitive, but he didn't know what to do about it and, at heart, he may not have believed it was important. He was one of many managers I've met who seem to think that if you get good results it doesn't matter if a few people are bruised along the way. However, as a numbers person, he knew his turnover and retention rates were the worst in the company and that replacing people was costing his company real money. As I began coaching him, I asked how I could be most helpful, and John said, "I'd like to be more of a people person."

If you've coached people for a while, you're probably asking the same question I asked myself at the time: How possible is that? Can someone at midlife really learn to think, feel, and act fundamentally differently toward people than he or she always has? Is being a people person something you can learn? Or is it a fundamental disposition and set of personality characteristics hardwired from birth or learned during the formative stages of human development and not very learnable beyond early adulthood? I told him that that kind of change in personality was unlikely but that if he were highly motivated he could learn how to *behave* more like a people person, and he said, "Fine. Give me some tips."

I was skeptical that behavioral tips would lead to sustained changes in his behavior, but he proved me wrong. He was initially motivated to change primarily because he wanted to improve his managerial ratings. I had hoped that his primary driver would be improving his relationships with his staff members. It was telling enough that he was mostly concerned about improving his managerial ratings. Surprisingly, however, in the course of using my tips to modify his behavior toward people, he learned how to work more effectively with them and came to see the value in it. In the year I coached him, his numbers did improve, and he became more aware of the people he was managing and more sensitive to their needs and feelings. So he taught me something important, namely, that managers often want to do the right things with people—even if not always for the best of reasons—but they don't know how. They have the will but not the skill.

In the past thirty years, I have coached thousands of managers, leaders, and executives in the world of work. During that coaching, I've learned that some managers have an intuitive grasp of people and know how to work with them, but many managers don't. Most would agree that having good relationships with the people they manage is crucial, but they are busy and don't find the time for relationship building. Many of them can't see their own blind spots so they don't know what they don't know about relating to people. Some know what they should be doing but lack the skill to do it, so they avoid it. What they need is practical advice on what to do and how to behave in ways that make their people more satisfied, more engaged in their work, more committed, and more productive. That's the ideal outcome, isn't it?

What Managers Want

Before I talk about what employees want, let's talk about you. As a manager of people, what do you want?

You probably want people who are competent and skilled at their jobs, people who are engaged and committed, loyal and hardworking. No doubt you want them to work well on their own but also work collaboratively with others. It's best if they are good team players, know how to apply themselves, have good ideas, and contribute substantially to the team's and the organization's success. You hope they have good people skills and get along well with clients or customers as well as fellow employees.

You probably want them to be diligent, keep their commitments, get things done on time, and achieve high-quality results in whatever they are doing. You also want them to be honest, fair, even-tempered, friendly, and attentive to detail. Finally, you want them to respect you, have a positive attitude, give and accept feedback graciously, resolve issues quickly, and leave their personal problems at home. This is the heaven scenario.

The hell scenario is about employees you don't want: These are employees who are competent but don't apply themselves; who are skilled at some things but unskilled at others (and don't seem motivated to learn); and who are disengaged, disloyal, and hardworking only when they choose to be. They don't work well on teams, don't get along with others; they upset or anger your clients or customers from time to time, have memory lapses, don't get the details right, show up late for meetings (if they show up at all), don't do what they should, don't get things done on time (and always have excuses), and don't produce the kind of quality you expect. They are dishonest or operate in shades of gray; are sometimes cranky, unfriendly, or distant; are occasionally disrespectful to you (usually behind your back); react to feedback as if you're throwing acid in their face; engage in destructive conflict with other people; and bring their personal problems to work and obsess on them ad nauseum (while the work is not getting done). Worse, their negative attitudes do more than darken the skies above their own heads—they spread their negativity to others. These hellcats are very high maintenance, and at the end of a day of managing them you go home feeling exhausted, angry, and depressed.

If you have managed people for any length of time, you have undoubtedly managed people fitting both descriptions. The former are a delight; the latter are a nightmare. No matter how good a manager you are, you will sometimes have or inherit "hell scenario" employees. They are out there, and even the finest managers sometimes have fits with people who are not motivated, don't care, take every advantage, push the boundaries, and are just plain awful to work with. Not everyone enjoys working, wants to contribute meaningfully, and has a "heaven scenario" disposition. Of course, the situation is more complex than people's personalities and attitudes. If it were that simple, we could simply give job candidates personality tests and weed out those who don't match the desired personality profile. (Some companies do this now, but even their success at selecting new hires with the right psychological and skill fit is limited. Creating a great workforce is partly about selecting people with the right attitudes and potential and partly about how you treat them once they are on the job.)

How you and your company behave toward the people who work for you has a lot to do with how those people will behave on the job. Rotten eggs are sometimes just plain rotten and are best disposed of, but most people who work for you are competent, have goodwill, and are reasonably easy to get along with. However, they are human beings and will therefore have a complicated set of attitudes, motives, expectations, and needs—just as you do as their manager.

You will never get what you want from everyone who works for you, no matter what you do. There are no magic wands for turning deadbeats into darlings. Still, you can do a lot to create a well-functioning team of committed, positive people, and that's what this book is about. The secret is deceptively simple: *to get the most from the people you manage, you have to treat them the way they want to be treated.*

What People Want

Most motivation studies by industrial psychologists take an understandably broad look at why people work and what motivates them to work harder and commit to their organizations. Although these studies usually show that the relationship with the supervisor is an important factor in work satisfaction and motivation, they don't address what people want from that relationship. To be most helpful to managers such as John, I needed to understand what people at work feel they need from their relationships with their managers. To find out, in 2004 and 2005 I conducted a study on that topic through the Lore Research Institute. Nearly five hundred people in a variety of businesses were asked what they wanted in their relationships with managers, peers, and close family or friends. The results revealed a number of significant differences in people's needs. Throughout this book, I will talk about what I learned from this research, and especially how it pertains to what people want from their managers and how managers can respond to their needs. For details on the research study, see the Appendix.

Chapter 1 introduces the results of the research on what people want from their relationships. It cites the list of needs from the most highly rated—trust—to the least highly rated among the top seven. As I report those seven needs, I give specific ways you can respond, including behaviors and attitudes you can adopt, to help to build relationships. As with all chapters in the book, Chapter 1 ends with a summary list of tips for improving your relationships.

Since the key point in all the research is trust, which was ranked at the top of virtually everyone's list of needs, Part I comprises five chapters that focus on trust and what it takes to build it. I conclude that to build trust you have to be worthy of trust, set the right tone for constructive relationships, be sensitive toward others, be respectful toward them, and make it personal (in appropriate ways). When you do those things, you address all the relationship needs listed in Chapter 1.

Chapter 2 discusses what you have to do to build a foundation of personal and professional trust with the people who work for you. Chapter 3 describes the fundamental attitudes and behaviors that underlie good interpersonal relationships. It introduces the concept of grace as it applies to relations with other people.

Chapter 4 describes what people who are naturally sensitive to others do well. Empathy is easier to understand in concept than it is to practice, especially for people who are not inherently empathetic. To be a good manager of people, however, you must understand how to sense what others are feeling, how to truly step into their shoes and see things from their perspective, and how to reflect their feelings back to them. Writers on the subject of emotional intelligence consider empathy a core competency.

Chapter 5 is about understanding and showing respect for people's rights and their differences. In collections of anecdotes published about bad bosses, one of the most frequent abuses reported is the boss who disrespects employees in various, often unbelievable ways. Respecting others is a foundation for building good relationships with employees.

Chapter 6 is about how you make employee relationships appropriately personal by being curious about people's lives and finding richness in each person's circumstances and journey. The best manager-employee relationships have the right degree of familiarity and human connection.

But understanding how to treat others is not enough. In addition to how you treat others, to be on solid ground in your relationships with other people, you must also have a good self. That is, you must respect yourself, keep an even keel, and avoid the dark side of behavior. That's what Part II is about.

Chapter 7 reflects what Anne Morrow Lindbergh once said: "When one is out of touch with oneself, one cannot touch others." To respect yourself, you have to take care of your own needs, trust your instincts, and protect your own personal and psychological space. To some extent, being a manager makes you an object of public scrutiny, however limited that "public" might be, and it can overwhelm you if you don't respect yourself, maintain appropriate boundaries, and teach others how to treat you.

Chapter 8 gives ways you can maintain your balance, stay centered, learn not to respond when your hot buttons are pushed, and be comfortable with yourself in the midst of turmoil. Finally, Chapter 9 discusses how to avoid some common bad behaviors, including bullying, threatening, and intimidating others. This chapter describes some of the most recent research on managers who fail because of "dark side" behaviors.

The Afterword talks about how to enjoy the journey. For too many managers, managerial work is a mixed blessing. Managerial work should be interesting and enjoyable, but in fact it leaves many managers depressed and worn out. In this section, I talk about what you can do to make the journey enjoyable and worthwhile for you and the people you manage, even if you don't naturally enjoy managing people.

Finally, the Appendix describes my research on what people want from their relationships. As it shows, my initial study of people's relationship needs led to a second, more comprehensive study that yielded the findings I describe throughout the book. The Appendix includes findings about what specific groups of people—men and women, people of different ages, introverts and extroverts, spiritual and nonspiritual people, managers and nonmanagers and more—want from relationships. You'll see the details of those findings there in chart format for easy reference.

Throughout the book, I offer concrete suggestions for improving your relationships. The main focus is on relationships with employees, but the tips can apply to virtually any type of human relationship.

As one writer on employee retention, Paul Michelman, says, "much of the responsibility for retention rests with individual managers and their ability to employ Grade A people-management and motivation skills. Leaders who can enable meaningful and fulfilling work experiences for their teams are much more likely to win loyalty and retention—especially when times are tight and monetary rewards may be slim."[1] The purpose of this book is to help you learn how to be more effective at managing your interpersonal relationships with employees—and how, consequently, to develop a stronger, more committed team of people who find their relationship with you not only motivating but inspiring as well.

I have one caveat as we begin. The suggestions I offer are ones that should work in most cultures most of the time. However, human beings, and the cultural and organizational contexts in which they interact, are infinitely complex. It's likely that some of my suggestions will not be appropriate for every person in every culture every time. There are simply too many variations for any book to address, so I would ask you to consider the intent behind the suggestion and reflect on the culturally appropriate equivalents if something doesn't seem right for your culture or some of the individuals you manage.

1 | What People Want Most

You can improve your relationships with other people if you better understand what they want from their relationship with you. In this chapter, I will summarize the research on what people want and begin offering suggestions for improving your relationships with others, particularly with your employees.

Although some of my suggestions may seem self-evident and too basic to some readers, in nearly thirty years of coaching managers and teaching interpersonal skills programs, I have seen countless cases where the ideas and behaviors I suggested, although they seemed like common sense, were clearly not self-evident to some managers and came as revelations when I suggested them. What is basic to one person is a new learning—or *re*-learning—for someone else. In this chapter and throughout the rest of the book, I will offer best practices in interpersonal behavior that will make a difference if you are not already doing them. I hope you will find a few gems (or reminders) that will help improve your relationships with your employees as well as with the other people in your life.

The Top Seven Needs

My research showed the following as the top seven needs people have in their relationships:

1. **Feeling that others trust me**

   Trust is the most fundamental relationship need. Without trust, there will not be much of a basis for a relationship at all, especially at work, where relationships are for the most part not complicated by long family or personal histories. People also want to feel that they can be honest with others and that others will be honest with them.

2. **Feeling challenged; feeling as if I am growing**

   With rare exceptions, people are not content in trivial, boring, or stagnant jobs. They don't want to do the same things day after day, month after month, year after year. They need to feel that their work is challenging and that they are developing their skills, capabilities, and possibilities. For most people, a satisfying career consists of a series of increasingly challenging roles and responsibilities.

3. **Feeling good about myself**

   Self-esteem can come from a constellation of qualities and accomplishments: appearance, intelligence, talents, autonomy, integrity, awards, titles, positions, job responsibilities, membership in special groups, acceptance or recognition by important others, and so on. The elements that constitute high self-esteem for each of us vary considerably, depending on our background and life experiences, and those elements evolve as we grow and develop and as our expectations change.

4. **Feeling competent and skilled**

   People want to be expert at something, however modest that something might be, because it's critical to how they define themselves and how they develop and sustain self-esteem.

5. Being appreciated for who I am and what I do

People want others to recognize their accomplishments and hold them in high regard. Even beyond simple recognition, however, people want to feel pride in who they are and be genuinely accepted for what they contribute. Acceptance and appreciation are essential to feeling part of a community.

6. Feeling excited about what I am doing

People want to be energized and enthused. In virtually every part of our lives we search for excitement for the simple reason that it's more fun than the alternative. We live for that adrenaline rush, whether it comes from scaling mountains, running rivers, watching a suspenseful movie, dancing with a loving partner, having a lively debate, closing a remunerative deal, or launching a new project.

7. Feeling involved in activities that matter to me

People want to feel that their time on earth is relevant, that they are contributing to something they believe in. Nothing is worse than going through the motions and feeling that you're wasting your time.

Clearly, some of these relationship needs are interrelated. Feeling that others trust you helps you feel good about yourself, contributes to feeling appreciated for who you are and what you do, and is an essential condition for feeling that you can be honest with others and they will be honest with you. Likewise, feeling challenged and successfully meeting those challenges is an enabler for feeling competent and skilled and for feeling excited about what you are doing. We might argue, in fact, that all these relationship needs are ultimately about developing and sustaining an identity of merit. In short, they may all be about having high self-esteem. Nonetheless, the differences between these needs are fruitful areas for reflection, because managers can do specific things to help their employees meet these needs.

Help People Feel That You Trust Them

What people want most from relationships is to feel trusted. They want others to rely on their honesty, character, and dependability; to have confidence in them; to entrust them with responsibilities; to have faith in their ability to get the job done; to assume that they are trustworthy and responsible. Someone once said that people of genius are admired, people of wealth are envied, people of power are feared, but only people of character are trusted. The essence of this relationship need is clearly character, but in a business context it's also about competence.

We trust people who deserve to be trusted because they are of high character and they get the job done well. They've earned our trust and demonstrated through their behavior and performance that they are capable, responsible, and dependable. That said, I've met a number of managers who are untrusting by nature or behave as though they are untrusting. They don't delegate responsibility, they micromanage, or they double- or triple-check people's work to an extent that is stultifying and demeaning. You can certainly trust too much and be disappointed, but the greater error is to not trust enough. People tend to live up (or down) to our expectations of them. If you trust people, most will respond by being more worthy of that trust, and vice versa.

Here are ways to show employees that you trust them.

Be Trustworthy Yourself

Trust is a delicate thing. It's hard to gain and easy to lose, especially for those of us in management roles, because people read so much into our behavior and words and may assume intentions that may not reflect our intent at all. I've been reminded many times that trust is a manager's most important asset. I'll have much more to say about this in Chapter 2.

Give People Your Trust

Generally speaking, you should assume the best of people and give them your trust. Unless you have evidence that they don't deserve trust, give them the benefit of the doubt. If you make wise hiring decisions, you should avoid getting untrustworthy people on board, but this is clearly not always possible. When someone proves to be undeserving, get rid of him or her. In environments where you've had trust issues surface, make your expectations about trustworthy behavior clear to everyone and recognize and reward the people who are most trustworthy. When you establish a high standard, people will be clearer about what you expect and what gets rewarded.

Of course, you can't trust everybody, and we all make hiring mistakes, no matter how careful we are. Sometimes the person you expect to be most trustworthy is the one least deserving of it. Still, if you have a suspicious nature and are fundamentally untrusting, everyone will know that, and you will spoil some otherwise great employee relationships.

Ask People What They Think

You show trust in people when you solicit their ideas and are curious about and interested in them and what they think. Outstanding managers solicit ideas in a variety of ways. Most effective is talking to people one-on-one and asking for their opinions. E-mails to groups of people are clearly impersonal and don't build trust like an individual sit-down with someone. If you don't have the time for individual meetings, schedule brainstorming meetings with groups of employees. Write down the best ones and give individual feedback afterward on how useful those ideas were. Then act on the ideas if you can. Acting on ideas and giving credit for them is much more effective than simply paying lip service to them.

Validate People's Contributions

An important way to show people that you trust them is to validate their contributions. First, be aware of what they've contributed (you may need to step back and reflect on this). Then acknowledge their contributions, publicly if possible. Adopt their ideas, giving appropriate credit, and ask them to contribute more. Sometimes, all you have to do is say, "That's a great idea." Clearly, you must be sincere if you say this. Managers who are inauthentic in giving praise create skepticism and destroy their own credibility. However, the greater error, in my experience, is not noticing what people have contributed, not validating their contributions, and therefore not conveying that you trust them.

Give People Meaningful Responsibilities and the Latitude to Fulfill Them

One of the best ways to convey trust is to give someone a substantive and meaningful assignment and the latitude needed to carry it out. To show your trust, the assignment has to be meaningful, and you must give the person the authority and resources to complete it successfully. If you're not sure the employee is completely up to the task, provide coaching for him or her.

Enable People to Make or Contribute to Key Decisions

You show trust when you delegate the authority to make key decisions—and then stand by those decisions. When it's not appropriate to delegate the authority, ask people to contribute to the decision-making process and then listen to and honor their contributions, whether or not they are reflected in the final decision. When you withhold all the decision-making authority, you send the signal that you don't trust any of your people. You have to be willing to let go of some meaningful decisions to help people feel trusted.

Avoid Micromanaging, Nitpicking, and Hovering

One of the most ineffective managers I've ever been asked to coach was a woman who micromanaged to an extraordinary degree. She dove into the most minute details of everyone's work; demanded time-consuming reports of people's activities; and worked around her management team, often changing her managers' decisions without informing them and giving assignments to their direct reports, which made her managers' lives complete chaos. You show absolutely no trust when you micromanage people.

Give People Assignments with Some Degree of Risk or Challenge

You show trust in people when the assignments you give them have some element of risk or challenge. If every assignment you give them is routine and safe, you convey little trust. But if the consequences of failure are moderately high and you ask them to accept the assignment and don't subsequently micromanage them, you convey substantial trust. Of course, you shouldn't give people assignments that are well beyond their capabilities, but giving assignments that force them to stretch to a reasonable degree will be motivating and demonstrates trust.

I was once on a client assignment with two colleagues who had considerably less experience than I did. The more senior of my colleagues, Karen, knew more than she thought she did and was ready, in my mind, to take the lead on these kinds of assignments, although she lacked the confidence to do so and would not have accepted the lead role without having a lot more experience. We were on-site with the client for a week and as it so happened on Monday morning I woke up with a sharp pain on my left side. That pain turned out to be a kidney stone that required an operation, so I wound up in the hospital all week. Karen was forced by that circumstance to step into the lead role, and she performed brilliantly. After that, she was fully confident, and the client was confident about her.

I knew she would perform well and told her that as I was heading off to the emergency room. During the week, when she visited me in the hospital, we'd talk about how she was doing and what she needed to do the next day. Every time we spoke, I expressed my confidence in her ability to do the job. Things might have been different had I not been incapacitated. She would have resisted taking the lead, but she would eventually have gotten there with persistence on my part. It's important to note, however, that what I didn't do was call in a more experienced consultant to handle the job. I trusted her to do it, and she did well. It was a transforming experience for her.

Give People the Opportunity to Represent Your Group or Company

When you ask people to host customers, clients, or other VIPs, or to represent the company at a trade show or convention, you convey trust in them. You may need to coach them, give them mentors or guides, or provide training to build their skills, but few things are as motivating to most people as representing the company in some public forum.

Let People Own Their Jobs

One of the managers I coached enabled his teams to define their own jobs, and he soon found that they had eliminated a number of tasks, streamlined work flow, and found ways to enhance not only their own work processes but the way team members worked together. They eliminated several positions when people retired or were transferred out of the group and became considerably more productive—all without the manager's direct involvement. People are creative and resourceful when you trust them to use their heads and do what they think is best.

Give People Flexible Work Arrangements or Schedules

If possible, make job sharing, flextime, and similar programs available to your employees. Programs such as these, which are now standard in many companies, began as responses to the needs of a more diverse workforce and were implemented by creative managers. And if you can, get rid of the time clocks. They may still be necessary for accounting purposes in companies with hourly workforces, but they do not convey trust.

Involve People in New-Employee Selection and Orientation

One of Southwest Airlines' most innovative employee-involvement programs allows employees to participate in selecting new employees and orienting them to the workplace. Asking employees to participate in these human resource processes helps build a sense of ownership and pride and conveys trust.

Ask People to Coach or Mentor New Employees

You can ask the people who have the skills and interest to coach or mentor others. Coaching and mentoring build upon people's expertise and show that you trust them enough to show others how to do the job right. They become standard bearers for the culture and the group.

Let People Be the Voice of Your Group or Company

You can ask trusted employees to speak for your group or company with customers or the media. You'll want to be selective here, but the people you put in front of customers, especially important customers or the media, feel a tremendous amount of trust and will normally rise to the occasion. To build your own trust and their confidence, you may need to have them apprentice in this role for a while with more experienced people before turning them loose.

Help People Feel Challenged

I once observed a civil service employee in a government office sit in his cubicle for an hour at the end of a day, rearranging things on his desk, moving pencils around, and occasionally reading something on a bulletin board beside his desk—but doing no work. At precisely 4:45, he picked up his briefcase, which he hadn't opened in the time I observed him, and left the room. I later saw on the flextime schedule that his workday ended at 4:45. He had checked out much earlier, and I'm sure he was also marking time until his retirement, which may have been years away. It was a monumental waste of human potential.

Without challenge, people stagnate. The best will motivate themselves, pursue their own challenges, and leave if the working environment is as pathetically dull as the government office I observed, but it's a manager's responsibility to ensure that the working environment is challenging, that people can learn and grow continuously.

Here are some ways to help people feel challenged.

Ensure That People Have Meaningful, Purposeful Work

Tedium and boredom come from doing the same thing the same way every day. People can endure the monotony for a while, but eventually it deadens the spirit and demotivates them. To create the right level of challenge for people, notice when their learning stops, when they have mastered the job and are growing bored or complacent. You may need to redefine their positions so they are learning new things and capitalizing on their real strengths. In my own company, I've done this more times than I can count. You find a good person, but that person turns out to be great at some things you hadn't envisioned and not so good at the things you hoped she might do. So you move her to a new role or change her job so she is doing what she loves to do most and she consequently does best—and where she has the capacity for growth and greater challenge as you increase her more-focused responsibilities.

Explain the *Why*

Any work, even menial work, can become more challenging and meaningful when people understand why you are asking them to do it—how it fits into the bigger picture, why it's necessary, how it contributes to the company in some way. Good people thrive on context and wither in its absence. To challenge them, ask them to examine their work process, flow, or product and come up with a better way: "How can we do this better, faster, or cheaper?" Most people love that kind of problem solving.

Give People New Opportunities

Assign people to task forces, project teams, cross-functional teams, problem-solving committees, and the like, or give them new, more challenging assignments, or rotate them to new positions. To thrive, people need stimulation and change. Don't ask the best ones to do the same thing too long. They will wither or, more likely, will leave you for more challenging opportunities.

Constantly Challenge People to Find Improvements

One of the finest managers I've ever known was virtually a challenge machine. He walked around to people's desks, or gathered small groups at lunch, or polled team members during projects and asked questions such as the following.

▪ How can we do it better?

▪ What problems or opportunities am I not seeing?

▪ What are the top two things we should change?

- If you were using our products, what would you like most? What would frustrate you?
- What would delight you or frustrate you about working with us if you were one of our customers?
- How could we streamline the process?
- How could we provide a higher level of satisfaction for our customers?
- What more can we do to differentiate ourselves from the competition?

As you might imagine, his group was one of the finest, highest-performing, most creative groups in his company. The best way to challenge people—and yourself—is to strive for continuous improvement and be not only open to new ideas but practically beg for them. The corollary to this is that you have to jolt those who have become complacent. Some people are dead on their feet and will stay that way no matter what you do. Find a way for them to leave. With everyone else, stimulate them to do more, do it better, and do it in less time. You may be able to stimulate them by adding them to high-performing teams and using peer pressure to get their juices flowing. Just beware of the potential negative effect on your best team members if they continue to drag lead weights around. If that happens, save the team.

Continuous improvement programs, such as Six Sigma, are valuable, but nothing is a substitute for your own leadership. If you are curious, have a questioning style, and strive constantly for continuous improvement and learning, then you will feed your people's need to be challenged whether or not you have programs such as Six Sigma in place.

Don't Put Roadblocks in Front of Your High Performers

I recall one manager whose ego appeared to be threatened whenever anyone who worked for him took the initiative or came up with a creative idea. Rather than encouraging innovation and continuous improvement, he insisted on reviewing ideas to death and resisted changes that he had not initiated himself. Some of the good people working for him gave up. Others left. I told him that it shouldn't matter where the great ideas come from. Encourage them, implement them, give credit where it's due, and celebrate your innovators. They make you look good. More important, they help improve the overall performance of your team.

Challenge People to Defend Their Ideas and Find Proofs

Consulting firm McKinsey & Company creates a meritocracy of ideas and encourages people at all levels in the firm to speak up if they disagree with someone's point of view. Even the most junior McKinsey associate has an "obligation to dissent." This stimulating environment challenges everyone to stay sharp, think through problems and opportunities, be innovative, and work hard to discover the best ideas. You help people feel challenged when you create an environment that forces them to work harder to find the best solutions.

Insist That People Have Their Own Ideas

I worked with one manager who asked for ideas but never used them unless she appropriated them as her own. I've seen others who will invite suggestions and then debate them to death, which sends the clear message that they didn't really want those suggestions in the first place. To avoid bias, you have to demonstrate your openness to new ideas. And when you go into a meeting, don't bias the dialogue by telling people what you think. Just ask the questions "How would you approach this? What are your thoughts? How would you do it?"

Create a Self-Conscious Learning Environment

In a learning environment, problems and failures are expected and are acceptable as long as they result in learning. This is an environment in which learnings are discussed and debated and then codified and shared with other groups, an environment in which managers constantly ask, "What are we learning? How can we apply those learnings? What more do we need to learn?"

Consider periodically holding learning meetings where you ask, "What key things have we learned recently?" Capture those ideas, prioritize them in terms of the size of the positive impact on your group if you implement the learning and the cost/time requirements to implement. Look for quick, easy wins, but don't neglect the major-impact items that take more time to implement. Ask some people to assume responsibility for implementing key learnings.

Walk around on Fridays and ask people, "What did you learn this week?" If you do this consistently, they will understand that you want them to be continuous learners. When someone mentions something particularly good, have that person share it with others or act as a coach or mentor to others. Find ways to spread the knowledge and use it.

Insist on Development Plans for Everyone

One of the best ways to challenge people is to encourage them to develop themselves continuously. Have everyone in your group, regardless of position, create a development plan for himself or herself. Then find the kinds of learning and development activities that are best suited for each person and within your budget. Send people to training seminars or workshops, university education programs, or trade schools; find them coaches or mentors; or create cohort learning groups where they can help educate one another. Ensure that their development plans are specific, measurable, realistic, and timely. Then monitor the plans and adjust as people improve their skills and capabilities.

Help People Feel Good about Themselves

As a manager, you are in a key position to validate people's self-esteem. You can help raise it, and you can diminish it. The hierarchical difference between you and the people who work for you makes your position like that of a parent. You have considerable influence on their lives, and they know this. Of course, anyone with a healthy ego won't let your judgment of them affect their self-concept significantly, but you can powerfully influence their views of themselves based on your words and actions. People with developing egos (mostly younger workers) or those whose egos are fragile for whatever reason will look to you for considerable validation of their worth. You can literally make or break these people by being encouraging, supportive, laudatory, and kind, or by being indifferent, overly critical, discouraging, and cruel.

How you affect people's self-esteem revolves around one word: *respect.* Respect is about honoring basic human dignity, and it requires empathy—the ability to put yourself in others' shoes and recognize that they aren't so different from you. No matter what people's station or predicament in life, we are all human. To recognize the essential humanity in others is to accord them the respect they deserve as human beings.

I have met a number of people who failed to respect others. One was the most narcissistic person I've ever met. He thought so grandly of himself that no one else could measure up—and he let them know that. He frequently left colleagues and subordinates in tears and was bluntly critical to the point of cruelty. He would take pride in tearing people apart in front of others (and smile while doing it). Although he was impressive to clients because of his intelligence, he found it difficult to sustain collegial relationships, and no one wanted to work with him. People who show little respect toward others generally have low self-esteem themselves, although they might disguise it with bravado.

Disrespecting others is their attempt to compensate for their own feelings of inferiority.

Here are some simple, commonplace ways to help people feel good about themselves.

Feel Good about Them

You can help people feel good about themselves by feeling good about them yourself—a foundational attitude that will carry through in every one of your interactions with them. Maintain the threads of respect and humanity through your accumulated interactions with the people you manage. Assume that they are acting with good will and have benign intent and then treat them that way. If someone doesn't deserve it, you will know in time and can act. Meanwhile, treat everyone with equanimity.

Use the Minimum Forms of Respect and Courtesy Consistently

Say "please," "thank you," and "you're welcome" to people, and extend the basic courtesies such as holding doors open for them. The employees of Ritz-Carlton are told that they are ladies and gentlemen serving ladies and gentlemen, and this attitude pays big dividends to the luxury hotel chain because its employees behaviorally differentiate themselves from the employees in rival hotels. Ritz-Carlton understands that people will pay to be treated well. Similarly, smart managers know that the basic courtesies are visible signs of respect, and, given a choice, people would rather work for someone who respects them and honors their basic humanity.

Pay Attention to People and Listen to Them

When you pay attention to someone, you acknowledge that that person exists, that he or she is worth your time and has meaning in your life, even if only for a moment. Hear what people have to say. Don't interrupt a person while she is speaking to you, and don't dismiss her ideas out of hand. You still may not agree once you've heard the viewpoint, but absorb it first and show that you have considered it. At a minimum, acknowledge that you have heard the person.

Expect People to Succeed

The word *encourage* comes from the French word *coeur* (heart) and means literally "to fill the heart." When we encourage people, we fill their hearts and give them the strength to carry on. As a manager, you do a tremendous amount of that when you encourage people, expect them to succeed, and then give them the coaching, time, resources, and attention to accomplish what you know they can. If you aren't sure that they can do it, be careful what you communicate. If you openly express your skepticism, you show that you expect failure—which you are likely to get unless they are resilient enough to show you they can do it. If you truly don't believe someone can do something, talk them through it, brainstorm how they will overcome the obstacles they may not foresee, and coach them through it. But be wary about expressing open skepticism, even if you think it's being more honest.

Support People's Efforts

You help people feel good about themselves when you are there for them. Don't say, "I support you" and then be silent or absent. Give assistance that is active, demonstrative, visible, and effective. It isn't support unless the person receiving the support feels that it is. So show up, be a fan, write the letters, send the cards, make the phone calls, and so on.

Help People Feel Competent and Skilled

A weekend with four grandchildren reminded me how important it is for all of us to feel skilled. "Grandpa, look at me," a four-year-old pleads as she jumps into the pool and emerges with a huge smile because she's learned how to do a cannonball.

We all want to feel that we are capable, that we know how to do things and do them well—and that people we care about know how capable we are. We take pride in our skills and know-how. Our competencies are a huge source of self-respect and make us deserving of respect, recognition, and acknowledgment. We need this even more at work because our competence earns us not only peer recognition and the respect of our family and community but also job security, higher compensation, promotions, and career opportunities. Small wonder that people have such a high need to feel competent and skilled—and have their manager recognize that.

Here are some ways you can help people feel competent.

Most Important, Hire Competent People

For people to *feel* competent and skilled, you need to put them into positions where their existing skills match the requirements of the job. Although this point seems patently obvious, it's often difficult to accomplish because it's a moving target. As people grow and learn on the job, they become increasingly overqualified for their current position, and you may not have complete latitude to move them to new positions as their skills increase. Clearly, ideal employees are ambitious and want to grow. They become discontented once they become overqualified in their current roles, and you need to keep giving them more challenging assignments and roles requiring increasingly difficult skills, or at least different skills, to keep them engaged. The challenge for managers is to remain aware of people's increasing skill levels, give them challenging assignments and roles that require them to develop their skills, and then move them on to greater challenges once they have mastered their current ones.

Notice and Acknowledge People's Skills

I said above that you need to remain aware of people's skill levels, but you also need to notice and acknowledge people's skills. You will find it easier to be aware of people's skills and coach or counsel them during performance reviews, but it's equally important to recognize and praise people for their skills on a regular basis. Try to develop a skills mind-set in which you are constantly aware of the skills and competencies of those working for you. Be aware too of where and how they need to grow, and coach them on their development needs. Once they've mastered a set of skills, move them on to greater challenges.

Make Others Aware of Your People's Skills and Competencies

You strengthen relationships when you publicly acknowledge people and applaud them for their skills. By doing so, you tell people, first, that you noticed and, second, that you care enough and are proud enough of them to communicate your awareness and recognition to other people. Just be sure your praise is genuine and deserved. Most employees have very good "crap detectors" and will learn not to trust you if you are inauthentic in your praise or if you praise people for things they really aren't that good at.

Ask People to Train Less-Experienced Employees

I once had the pleasure of observing an eight-year-old granddaughter teaching her three-year-old brother how to do things. As I watched, I realized how natural an impulse this is for human beings. Virtually everyone is a teacher at heart, and you satisfy people's need to be recognized for their skills when you ask them to teach someone else. Moreover, teaching is the best way to learn. When people prepare to teach others, they have to think through the basics again, codify their understanding, consider how best to present the skill in an understandable way, and discover ways to teach that are practical and successful—in short, they have to relearn the subject and sharpen their own skills. It's a tremendous way to help people feel competent.

Invest in Ongoing Training and Development

Earlier, I said that it's important to create a self-conscious learning environment. You do this at the individual level when you invest in people's ongoing training and development. You not only build their skills, you also reinforce what they already know and help them feel competent and skilled in the ways they already are. Moreover, most people find learning deeply gratifying. To good, vital people it is as important as breathing.

Support People through Failure

People will fail, especially people who are challenging themselves to do new things. To help people feel skilled and competent, you need to support them through their failures to the extent that you can, although some failures are easier to support than others. My rule of thumb is that an initial failure of any kind (except one deriving from lack of integrity) is acceptable so long as the person learns from it and doesn't repeat it. If you are unaccepting of failure, you discourage risk taking and foster an environment in which failures are hidden and people do not speak candidly or learn self-consciously.

When people fail at something, it's best to sit with them and say, "Well, *that* didn't work. What did we learn from it? How would you do it differently next time? How can we ensure that that doesn't happen again? What would help you avoid that sort of thing in the future?" Questions like these help calm the situation, reduce anxiety, and turn a negative into a positive learning experience. When people see that you will support them through failures, you strengthen relationships and gain loyalty. You also gain employees who are willing to take risks and apply learning continuously.

Help People Feel Appreciated for Who They Are and What They Do

Appreciation lies at the core of self-esteem. It is important to feel good about yourself—to have healthy self-regard without the need for external validation—but appreciation from others is extraordinarily important to all but a few people. Beyond simple recognition, people want to feel accepted as themselves and valued for their contributions. Being appreciated means being accepted, recognized, and valued, and this really is at the core of what it means to be human. When we feel accepted, we are free to be genuine, free to celebrate ourselves, and free to embrace not only our own differences but others' differences as well.

In short, acceptance means freedom. Anyone who has ever experienced prejudice will attest to the stultifying effect it has on their sense of liberty. People want to be accepted and appreciated regardless of their gender, race, religious preference, class, national origin, or sexual orientation. Being accepting of everyone is difficult for many people because we are tribal by nature. We learn early on that there is an "in crowd" and an "out crowd" and that the beliefs and practices of groups unlike ours are wrong and perhaps evil. The "in crowd" reinforces its specialness by excluding those who don't belong for one reason or another. From the earliest games we play as children where sides are chosen, we learn about social class and being included or excluded. Children don't have the maturity to understand the causes and effects of social groupings, but as adults we should be mature enough to comprehend those effects and wise enough to make choices. Accepting people is a choice we make, as is not accepting people.

As the manager of a group, you have special standing as the "tribal leader," and you strongly influence the norms in the group about accepting people and appreciating them for who they are and what they do.

Here are some ways you can help people feel appreciated.

Be Respectful toward Everyone and Accept Them for Who They Are

To have any hope of creating strong working relationships with your employees, you absolutely must treat them with respect, which means what you would expect it to mean: accepting and even celebrating diversity, speaking positively about people when they aren't around, not making or tolerating jokes at someone's expense, being respectful of legitimate lifestyle choices, and so on. Joking is particularly tricky because it's a form of bonding between some people, but to others it can seem disrespectful and abusive, and it carries far more weight when it comes from a manager. Use sensible caution and avoid making or perpetuating jokes.

Establish a Respectful Environment in Your Group

As a manager you strongly influence the norms of behavior in your group. You set the boundaries and show what is or is not acceptable. Whenever a hostile work environment exists in a company, management is to blame. Period. So create an environment of zero tolerance of discriminatory or hostile behavior. If bad behavior occurs, deal with it firmly, fairly, and quickly. To help people feel appreciated for who they are and what they do, you must establish cultural and behavioral norms in your group in which everyone is valued and respected and no one is abused, singled out, made fun of, or discriminated against because of who they are. It's as simple as that. Appreciation begins with respect.

Honor People's Preferences

Sometimes, the Thomases of this world prefer to be called Thomas rather than Tom. When you hire someone or otherwise add new employees to your group, ask what they prefer to be called and, to the extent you can, honor their preferences on how they dress, what personal things they keep in their work areas, and so on. Clearly, some companies offer more latitude than others in how people dress and organize their work areas. Where you are able to respect people's preferences, you will develop stronger relationships with them and be repaid by greater loyalty.

Publicly Recognize People's Successes and Contributions

In managers' 360-degree assessments, *recognition* is frequently near the bottom in rankings of manager strengths. No matter how much we think we do give recognition, employees often want more, and in my experience employees aren't asking for more than they deserve, just more than they usually get. The tricky part of public recognition is doing it in a way that doesn't appear to diminish those not being recognized and, in team-based or matrixed organizations, to ensure that you are recognizing the right people for the right things and not inadvertently leaving out a deserving person. So think through it carefully and ensure that proper due is given to the right people. The ceremonies need not be elaborate. An informal lunch with pizzas and salads brought in is usually very effective.

The recognition should be symbolic and memorable in some way. In my company, Lore International Institute, we use the meerkat as a metaphor for cooperation and collaboration. The meerkat, a creature that lives in the Kalahari Desert, is considered one of the most cooperative animals on earth. Lore employees refer to themselves as meerkats, and the most esteemed award anyone can receive is the Meerkat Award, which recognizes superior team members. It is awarded only in public ceremonies and with great fanfare. It's also awarded sparingly, so the people who receive it are renowned for their collaborative spirit. The award itself is a statue of a group of meerkats on a wooden pedestal—all looking in different directions for their mutual protection. The symbolism of this public recognition runs deep in my company, and it conveys more than the recognition of an individual—it is also symbolic of the company culture and reflects our operating principles. Meaningful awards do a tremendous amount for teaching and perpetuating the culture and for recognizing deserving members of the team.

Show Appreciation One-on-One, Too

Private recognition can also be meaningful to people, because people appreciate that you make the effort to stop by and praise them. And some people prefer personal and private recognition to public events where they might feel embarrassed or "on display." Introverts often prefer individual appreciation, but it depends on the person, and you have to know enough about your people to know what works best for each of them. In any case, taking the time to congratulate or praise people at their desks, in the hallway, or in the parking lot can strengthen relationships and make people feel appreciated.

Make It a Point to Recognize Someone Every Day

If you are like me and don't often think to recognize people, make a point of recognizing someone every workday. You might even ask your assistant or human resources manager to know who is deserving of praise and remind you to do it. I keep a supply of thank-you cards in my office for just such occasions.

Say "Nice Job" Once in a While—Even for Normal Work

The work doesn't have to be earthshaking for it to deserve praise. When people do their jobs well, they deserve a "nice job."

Keep Your Ego in Check and Don't Compete with Your People

I once coached an executive who took delight in hazing the young people in his office. No matter how well they did something, he found a way to joke about it or ridicule them in some way. He told me that he was just giving them a hard time, and they knew he was just joking around. What he wanted to accomplish, he said, was to push them constantly to do better. "You can't let them get a big head," he said. When parents do this sort of thing, they can crush a child's spirit and make the child feel that nothing he or she ever does is good enough. The same is true of managers whose good-natured banter is more deflating than inflating.

Even if you did it better in the past or could have done it better, even if you are smarter or know more than they do, bragging rights are irrelevant. Don't compare employees to you or compare their achievements to what you have achieved; compare them to themselves. If you say, in effect, "that's nothing," you make them feel worthless and diminish what they did accomplish, however great or small it might be. It's best in recognizing people to have a generous heart and a kind spirit.

Help People Feel Excited about What They Are Doing

People want to be stimulated by their work. They want it to have meaning and purpose. They want to be charged up. One of Lore's operating principles is to have fun, but I frequently tell people that we don't mean having beer bashes on Friday afternoons. We mean having good *professional* fun. If our clients and our work excite you, if you are enthusiastic about the work we do, then you belong here. If not, you should go somewhere else where you'll be more excited about what they do.

Excitement is contagious, but not everyone will catch the bug, so you will need to match the people to the project. You need to ensure that the people you hire or the ones who transfer to your group are authentically excited about the kind of work you do. Unless they are genuinely enthused about your products or services, clients or customers, workplace, and culture, you may not be able to do much but offer them extrinsic rewards to find excitement in your group.

Here are ways to help people feel excited about what they are doing.

Be Passionate Yourself

There's an old saying in Texas: you can't light a fire with a wet match. If you are dull and dispassionate yourself about the work your group is doing, don't expect others to create excitement (unless you have subordinates who are better, more inspiring leaders than you are). You have to be passionate about what you are doing. You have to manifest the energy yourself first. Then show your passion in your words, behavior, and decisions.

You might want to think of yourself as the CEO—the Chief Excitement Officer. Your job is to make coming to work fun, engaging, and interesting for those in your group. An essential component of this is envisioning a positive future, one in which people can believe that they are doing good work, that the work matters, and that they are headed toward success. People are fueled by optimism and stunted by pessimism, so when I am coaching managers who are inherently cynical or pessimistic, I suggest they park their cynicism at the door. It doesn't belong in management.

Appeal to People's Values and Passions

People are excited when they are doing something they care about and that they believe matters to other people. Find out what people find personally engaging, and involve them in your group's work if they find it interesting and energizing. If some people are not well suited for your team, move them out. For those who remain, be jazzed yourself, show your enthusiasm and commitment every day, communicate the purpose and meaning of the endeavor, have productive and creative ideas, and engage others to make them feel involved and relevant.

Make the Work Interesting—and New and Challenging

You want to make the work challenging, but some tedious work must be done. In my company, some people must process assessment forms, and others must produce workbooks and ship them to various locations. It's the same thing day after day. To give this kind of work meaning, you have to continually reinforce how important the work is to the firm and its clients. I've found it helpful to periodically ask the people doing this work what they find challenging and interesting about it. When you show interest in them and their work, you engage them and help them feel important (which they are!). You can also foster a sense of pride in them for having completed X number of assignments without an error.

You can also make work more interesting by challenging people to improve something about their work—the product, the process, the interactions with users of the product, and so on. When people feel more ownership for their work, they are more likely to sustain their engagement, take more pride in what they do, and convey their enthusiasm to others.

Finally, it helps to give people something new and challenging to do. Vary the assignments, add new dimensions to the work, or ask people to serve on new committees or take on new responsibilities. Periodically, you have to change people's work—and always in directions they consider better—to keep them engaged and energized over time.

Don't Be a Naysayer

Don't dampen people's spirits. I worked with one manager who felt that his role was to control everything and ensure that his people didn't go off on wild-goose chases, so he nitpicked every new idea and looked for the holes in people's arguments or the reasons why something wouldn't work. He took pride in calling himself the group's "reality checker," and he stifled not only new ideas but the sense that people could contribute in ways that might matter. Consequently, no one in his group loved coming to work. Many just gave up and did their jobs with the minimum of effort and care. The losses that company suffered—in terms of energy, commitment, quality, and caring for the customer—must have been staggering.

Celebrate Both the Journey and the Wins along the Way

You need to take time out periodically to celebrate. Celebrations create a time and place for excitement to be enjoyed openly, for the enthusiasm to become infectious. Celebrations signal, first, that you notice when something ought to be celebrated and, second, that you find it important to celebrate, to cherish the wins, whether they are great or small, and to recognize the group's successes. Celebrations add meaning and joy. But remember that *any effect diminishes with repetition.* Sending flowers to your significant other is powerful but not if you do it every day. The same is true of celebrations at work. Do them, do them well and with lots of fanfare, but don't do them too frequently. When you celebrate, make it special.

Make It a Great Place to Work

You help people feel excited about what they are doing when you strive to make your group or company a great place to work. Make the workplace a supportive, collaborative environment where people can be themselves and have good, professional fun. Set high standards and challenging goals, but allow people to figure out for themselves how best to achieve their goals.

You nourish people's spirits when you celebrate their dreams and make room for them to realize those dreams in a supportive, caring environment. *That* creates a great place to work.

Help People Feel Involved in Activities That Matter to Them

We are social creatures. We have a need for affiliation, for belonging. We want to be part of something greater than ourselves, something we care about. Beyond the need to be with others, to feel that we are not alone, we also need to have meaning in our lives, and that meaning comes in part from the groups of people we choose to associate with. It also comes from our work. We want to be engaged in an effort or enterprise we believe in, and we want to share the glory of the group's or team's successes. That's why so many people become avid fans of sports teams, why they feel such elation when the team wins and such crushing defeat and frustration when the team loses. It's why many people feel separation anxiety when they leave a school, company, team, or other group, and why retirement is difficult for many people.

The need for affiliation is a powerful positive force in our lives. For most people it means the warmth and security of friendship, the sanctity and unconditional acceptance of a loving family, the spiritual enrichment shared with fellow believers in a religion, and the unity of purpose and collegiality found in work teams and organizations. As managers, we need to be very aware of the strong need most people have for affiliation and the motivational power of creating strong bonds among people who work together.

Here are some ways to help people feel involved in activities that matter to them.

Help People Feel Passionate about the Work They Are Doing

People often don't see the big picture; they see only their small part of it, and their part may seem small, trivial, or inconsequential. You help them feel more passionate when you describe the bigger picture, when you talk about why it matters to someone, why it's important, how it contributes to something meaningful, what cause you all serve. The Ritz-Carlton Hotel Company does this by emphasizing its credo "We are ladies and gentlemen serving ladies and gentlemen," which elevates every Ritz-Carlton employee's role to something beyond the mere mechanics of cleaning rooms, delivering room service, or washing the laundry. In the best of companies, managers know how to put every role into perspective and help people feel that their contribution matters.

Once Again, Make It a Great Place to Work

As I discussed in the previous section, creating a great place to work can help people feel excited about what they're doing. It can also help people feel involved in work that matters to them. People who work in great companies or teams tend to reinforce one another's positive feelings about the place. Some of them will become role models for how to behave in the group. They will reflect the positive elements of the ideal culture (the one you want to be, in effect) and thus tend to align the actual culture (what people actually do and think). They will act as teachers and coaches to newer members and will use peer pressure to guide and correct those who are not aligned, which frees you from having to perform that role.

Involve People in Things That Matter to Them

Find ways to involve people in the work they are passionate about. Think about each person you manage. Talk to them informally and discover what they are most passionate about. At Lore we had one employee who was passionate about the Japanese martial art aikido and has a black belt in it, so we arranged for him to give weekly aikido classes during lunch hour. Other employees have become especially engaged in business development, research or publishing, or facilitating client meetings, and we've tried to ensure that they had those opportunities. Typically, there are constraints on what's possible for employee involvement, but do what you can within your constraints.

Of course, being involved means more than merely being included. Most people get engaged by taking an active part in the discussions, discoveries, and decisions. So give them *active,* participatory roles. Ask for their opinions. Better yet, involve them in the problem-solving and brainstorming parts of the discovery process so their minds are engaged more thoroughly. To *really* involve them, ask them to be responsible for all or some important part of the outcome. Give them the latitude to bring other people on board or to lead the team.

Keep People Informed

Give people more information rather than less. Overcommunicate in the areas that matter to them. Include people on mailing or distribution lists in the areas they are interested in or involved with.

Consider having town hall meetings where you give larger groups of employees information about what's happening and entertain their questions. This has worked very well for me, particularly in my willingness to answer any questions people in the group may have. Obviously, there may be some areas of sensitivity where you can't fully inform everyone about what's going on. I've found it best in those cases to be candid about that, and most people will understand and accept that. However, if you appear to be hoarding information or using it selectively, you are likely to breed mistrust.

These are just a few of the ways you can help people get what they want most from their relationships with their managers. Throughout the rest of the book, I will explore in depth how you can build trust; set the right tone; be sensitive to others; respect others; make relationships appropriately personal; respect yourself; keep an even keel; and avoid behaving badly in ways that can derail you, demotivate your employees, and damage your organization. Each chapter ends with a summary list of tips for improving your relationships as a manager.

Tips for Improving Your Relationships

1. Help people feel that you trust them.

2. Help people feel challenged.

3. Help people feel good about themselves.

4. Help people feel competent and skilled.

5. Help people feel appreciated for who they are and what they do.

6. Help people feel excited about what they are doing.

7. Help people feel involved in activities that matter to them.

PART 1 | In You I Trust

Trust is the foundation of every relationship, but it's especially important in manager-employee and colleague-to-colleague relationships where family ties and personal bonds are typically not in place. At work, relationships must be built on the basis of an employment contract or professional affiliation rather than shared interests, beliefs, or life experiences. The manager-employee relationship is unusual because of the power differential between the two roles.

We know from Chapter 1 that what employees want most from their relationships is to feel trusted. They also need to know that they can trust their managers. Trust arises from more than honesty and integrity; it is a complex feeling that emerges from a myriad of perceptions, observations, and interactions as employees work with their managers. Trust is built (or destroyed) with every one of the manager's actions, decisions, reviews, communications, and meetings. It is based both on what you as a manager do and what you don't do. Trust reflects employees' expectations as well as their experiences with other managers and organizations.

At heart, people trust you because you act with integrity and treat them respectfully and kindly. They will trust you more if you are sensitive toward them and personalize the relationship in appropriate ways. They will trust you if you understand and respect their boundaries and act with their best interests in mind. In Part I, I am going to explore the very practical ways managers can build and sustain trust with employees, and I will offer numerous suggestions for making yourself worthy of trust.

2 | Being Worthy of Trust

Nothing is more important to you, as a manager, than the perception people have of you as someone worthy of trust. When you have their trust, the people who work for you will work harder, be more productive and committed, take direction, receive coaching, and remain loyal in hard times. Without it, they will be suspicious of you, resent working for you, be less productive, and desert you at the first opportunity.

I am fortunate to have attended the United States Military Academy at West Point, where I learned and came to live by the cadet honor code, which states simply, "A cadet will not lie, cheat, or steal, or tolerate those who do." I graduated with hundreds of fine men who hold that high standard as a core belief. The reason so many of them became successful military, industry, and government leaders is that they are people who are worthy of trust. At West Point, we were taught that integrity is not conditional. A single violation of the honor code was sufficient for a cadet to be asked to leave the academy.

What does it take to build trust? Certainly it requires honesty, reliability, dependability, consistency, and all the other behaviors we associate with integrity—and unconditional adherence to these standards. However, trust also requires a generous and collaborative frame of mind, benign intent when dealing with others, open communication and, above all, authenticity. If you are collaborative, you foster camaraderie; if you are benevolent, you establish goodwill; if you communicate openly, you reduce fear; and if you are genuine, you overcome skepticism and convey your humanity.

When people start working with you, they have to size you up. They have to know whether you can be trusted, whether you are honest and truthful, whether you are a good person to work for, whether you will be fair, whether they can learn from you, and whether you will have their best interests at heart. Beyond talking to others about you, they will observe your behavior and form quick impressions about whether you are worthy of trust. Consciously or subconsciously, most people ask these kinds of questions about you:

- Are you honest? Do you always tell the truth? Can I believe what you tell me? Or do you sometimes shade the truth or deliberately mislead people for one purpose or another?

- Are you credible? Do you know what you are talking about? Can I trust you when you tell me something or act like an expert? Do I trust your opinions and judgments?

- Do you keep your commitments? If you make a promise, can I trust you to keep it? Or do you forget about promises or renege on them later?

- Do you own up to your mistakes and problems? Or do you blame others for your mistakes, hide them, or try to explain them away?

- Do you care about me as a person? Or am I just a "resource" to you? Do I matter to you beyond my ability to get good work done on time?

▩ Do you respect me and my work? Are you willing to recognize me for my contributions? Or do you try to take all the credit yourself?

▩ Do you have my interests and our organization's best interests at heart? Or do you act mostly out of self-interest? Are your decisions fair and impartial? Do you avoid favoritism or nepotism? Will you give me a fair shake if I do great work for you?

▩ Are you willing to go the extra mile for me and the organization? When things are tough, are you willing to pitch in?

▩ Will you back me up when I need you? If I'm being unfairly criticized or blamed for something I didn't do, will you defend me? Or will you throw me to the wolves?

▩ Do you use good judgment? Do you know when to push and when not to, when to ask me about something personal and when not to, when to examine my work and when to trust that my work products are excellent?

▩ Are you a good person? Do you treat people with equanimity and respect? Or do you joke or gossip about them behind their backs?

▩ Can I share personal information with you? Are you discreet with that information? Can I trust you to maintain confidences? Or will you use that information against me?

The questions I've just cited are an employee's way of determining whether you have that solidarity with them as a fellow human being or whether you consider yourself different or superior. As the old saying goes, "Power corrupts, and absolute power corrupts absolutely." When people work for you, they understand the power you have over them, and they want to know whether you will abuse that power or use it wisely and fairly. For you to be worthy of their trust, the answers to their questions must be reassuring. They have to know that you will treat them the way you would want to be treated if the roles were reversed and they were acting as your manager.

Be Unconditionally Honest

Several years ago I was asked to coach a manager who had very rocky relationships not only with her direct reports but with virtually everyone else in her company. She had survived to that point because she was brilliant and technologically savvy in a high-tech firm that needed her expertise. When I met her, I noted the remarkably low scores for integrity on her recent 360-degree assessment and asked if she was concerned about them. Very matter-of-factly she said, "No. I don't care about that. I lie whenever I have to." I had never met anyone as unashamedly unethical as this person. I told her I didn't think she would have much of a career if she kept that attitude, but she didn't care. She believed that the end justified the means, and she thought that the standards of integrity that everyone else applied to themselves were foolish and naive. They did not apply to her. Although I tried to be helpful to her, I was not surprised to learn later that the company had fired her.

Fortunately, most of the thousands of managers I've known are decent, honest human beings. They tell the truth as they know it and try to be straightforward with everyone, but sometimes they have to keep certain information confidential, or they have to be careful about what they say for a variety of other sensible reasons. In a managerial role, however, you can destroy trust quickly even if you are being totally honest but convey the *impression* that you're not being straightforward, are holding something back, are telling only part of the story, are shading the truth, or are otherwise telling people what they want to hear.

Some people, however, will always be a little suspicious of management, and they will look for evidence that you are not telling the whole truth. I once had an executive working for me who was like that. She tended to put the most negative spin on whatever I said and go into a death spiral, imagining what I was holding back but with no real way of knowing what it was. By the time I learned what was going on, she had driven issues to their extreme and was fomenting insurrection. She also had the unfortunate tendency to assume that I was thinking something, would react negatively to what she assumed, and would go downhill from there. I quickly learned that I had to overcommunicate with her, think carefully about how my words might be misinterpreted, and carefully observe her feelings and moods. As long as you must work with people who are inherently suspicious of you because you are a manager, you have to work hard to make sure they know you are being totally honest and straightforward with them.

Part of being honest is being candid, of course, but you have to be *sensitively* candid, and this can be tricky. The unvarnished truth can often be so hurtful to people that "telling it like it is" causes more problems than it solves. If your boss discusses a direct report of yours with you, berating her for the mistake she made, you would not want to be entirely candid about every word the boss said. But you must convey that the boss was unhappy about the mistake and be candid about what the person needs to do to rectify the situation and not let it happen again. What often works best in these situations is the sandwich technique: good news, bad news, good news. By framing the bad news within positive messages, the person delivering the news can feel better about himself or herself, and it helps the receiver as well. People who hate giving bad news are often very nurturing and hate to inflict pain on anyone. The sandwich technique helps them give bad news because it comes within their paradigm of being warm and caring people.

The bottom line is to be unconditionally honest but also sensitive. Choose the right words to convey the truth, and be sure to communicate openly and clearly. Poor communication is often the culprit behind distrust.

Be Credible

I worked with a manager several years ago who came up through the ranks as a technical expert in his field. He relished the role and loved being called upon for his knowledge and expertise. As he rose through the ranks, however, his span of authority came to encompass areas in which he was not an expert. But old habits are hard to change, and when he was asked technical questions about those new areas he tried to expound as though he knew what he was talking about. Of course, it didn't take long for people to see through his bravado, and they began to distrust much of what he said, even in areas where he had been an acknowledged expert.

To maintain your credibility, speak confidently about what you know and avoid speaking confidently about what you don't know. If you are making a fact-based judgment, say so. If you are giving an opinion based on intuition, say so. If you aren't sure, say so. If someone asks you a question and you don't know the answer, admit it and help them find someone who does. Don't assume that to be an effective manager you have to know everything, be wiser than everyone else, and be expert in all the areas you manage. (People who make this assumption often have low self-esteem; admitting ignorance or errors when they occur is actually a sign of strength.) The higher you go in an organization, the less likely it is that you will know as much as the real experts working for you. Calling upon the experts when necessary is a sign of genuine wisdom, and it shows that you are worthy of trust because you won't pretend to know something when you don't. Instead, you will help them find the right people with the right answers.

Keep Your Commitments

In my experience, few managers make promises they don't intend to keep, but some suffer from one of three syndromes that can make them

appear to be untrustworthy: they don't think they've made a commitment, they forget about the commitment, or they overcommit and can't
do everything they promised.

Some managers I've coached feel pressured to make commitments
and try to avoid doing so by carefully choosing their words: "Yes, I'll try
to get back to you by tomorrow noon at the latest." "That should be possible. Check with me in the morning." "At this point I don't see any reason why we can't commit to those dates." And so on. They think by
using vague qualifiers such as "I'll try," "should be possible," and "at this
point I don't see any reason why not," they are protecting themselves
and not really making a promise. I tell these wordsmiths that they are
implying a commitment and their careful use of language is just a
dodge. If you can't commit, don't.

Some managers are absent-minded types like me. In the press of a
busy day, it's easy to agree to something and earnestly make that commitment but forget about it when the next five minor crises occur. In
today's light-speed workplace, we can be overwhelmed by the sheer
number of demands, problems, opportunities, e-mails, and phone calls.
It's easy to say, "I'll get back to you" as a way to reprioritize an issue now
so you can handle two dozen more pressing ones and then forget to get
back to that person later. I've learned to keep track of my commitments
in my Blackberry so I don't forget the promises I've made. Unless you
have a sterling memory, you would do well to keep a written (or elec-
tronic) record of your commitments.

Finally, some managers overcommit. In their zeal to work harder,
get more done, or just keep their heads above water, they commit to
more than they can reasonably get done. Sometimes they overcommit
because they think it's expected of them (and, in fairness, it might be)
or because they genuinely believe they can do it all. Some people want
to please, so when people ask for something, they commit to it, believ-
ing at the time that they will find a way to keep the promise. Then

reality catches up with them. Feeling guilty later, they may become even more eager to please next time and make even more foolish commitments.

In order to handle these syndromes, think carefully about whether you really can keep the commitments you make *at the time you make them.* Don't be too quick to agree. But if you do agree, then move heaven and earth to keep the commitment. People have to know that they can depend on you to keep your word.

Keeping your commitments is especially important if you manage other managers. My research shows that, compared to nonmanagers, managers have significantly greater needs for loyalty, dependability, and commitment from those they work with. Three-quarters of the managers I surveyed said that loyalty from their boss was extremely important to them (only 2 percent said it was unimportant). People who are or have been managers also have a greater need for professionalism, teamwork, and collaboration from those they work with. They value from their boss the sorts of things you value in them: commitment, loyalty, professionalism, and cooperation.

Own Up to Your Mistakes

One of the managers I coached, Melissa, was smart but had a high need for control and presented herself as though she had a strong ego. She needed to appear infallible, so she would never admit when she was wrong. Shown evidence contrary to her point of view, she would say that people had misunderstood her and that the contrary point of view was what she had meant all along. When evidence accumulated that one of her projects was going badly and she had to radically change direction, she would tell people that she had deliberately started with that initial direction, knowing it was wrong, so the team would discover the right path through their mistakes. It didn't take long for the team to thoroughly distrust Melissa and dislike working for her.

"Being able to admit when you're wrong" is often cited in leadership models and assessments as one of the defining characteristics of effective leaders. Unless you can admit error, you hold yourself up to be infallible and create an impossibly high standard for yourself. Everyone, no matter how smart they are, has to be wrong some of the time. When you admit error, you show employees that you are human. Moreover, you show that you have character, that you are more interested in the best solution than in being right, and that you are capable of learning from your mistakes. People who are always right never learn. People who admit their mistakes, genuinely seek the best solutions (no matter where they come from or who has the idea), and visibly and self-consciously learn from their mistakes model the kinds of behaviors we see in learning organizations.

If you are right all the time and if you have all the best ideas, then you will stifle innovation, idea generation, and problem solving among your direct reports. If, on the other hand, you show a genuine willingness to explore ideas, to encourage innovation, and to listen to and accept the best that others have to offer, then you can create a vibrant team of people who love their work and will be encouraged to give more of what they have to offer. So admit it when you are wrong, have made a mistake, or have changed your mind. Do this genuinely. It cannot be faked. People will see through it if you are not sincere.

Furthermore, do not reinterpret the facts later to create the impression that you were right all along. Adopt the attitude that if your people had a different perception of reality than you did, then you failed to communicate clearly. It's your problem, not theirs. Apologize, clarify, seek common ground, and move on.

Care about People

In the Introduction, I talked about coaching John, who wanted to be more of a people person. One of the most common complaints about John was that he didn't care about the people who worked for him. He would see that someone was upset and ignore it. He would learn, for example, that one of his administrators had recently lost her mother and, instead of being compassionate and offering his condolences, he would ask that person when she was going to finish a task he'd assigned her. The people who work for you are not robots. They are living, breathing, and feeling human beings with hopes, dreams, and aspirations along with fears, anxieties, disappointments, and unfulfilled longings. If you want to have good relationships with your employees and coworkers, you have to recognize their humanity and care about them as human beings, not just as workers.

Be Available for People When They Need You

Remember that one of a leader's primary roles is to help everyone else do well—to engage them, motivate them, guide them, and give them a sense of purpose and meaning. For people to be motivated and focused, they have to be emotionally centered. They have to feel needed and cared about, and they have to feel good about working for you. You show caring by noticing how they're doing, asking what's wrong if something seems to be bothering them, and giving them help or emotional support when they need it. Yes, this could mean taking time out of your busy day or disrupting your schedule—and that is the price you must pay to maintain great relationships at work.

Be *in the Moment* with People
When They Are Distressed

Of course, it's helpful if you actually are a people person and enjoy being with people. I told John that I doubted I could turn him into a people person any more than I could give him a magic mushroom and make him four inches taller. However, I did teach him to *be in the moment* with people whenever he saw that someone was distressed, upset, unhappy, distracted, or otherwise not engaged and not behaving normally. In those moments, I told him, you have to set aside whatever else you are doing and focus on that person. Ask what's wrong and how can you help. If the situation appears to be sensitive, find a quiet, private place to talk.

Don't Avoid Dealing with People's Personal Issues

Some managers don't like dealing with personal issues. They're uncomfortable when someone is in distress, and they feel pressure to get the work done. But the plain fact is that we human beings are emotional creatures, and we occasionally become distressed. Life is sometimes messy. Show that you care, and deal with it.

Respect People's Work

You show respect for people's work when you leave them alone to do their work and don't interfere unless it's absolutely necessary to do so. When you give people the space to do their work and the latitude to decide how to do it best, you show that you respect their character and capacity to do the job well. Unlike micromanagers who nitpick details and make frequent midcourse corrections, you show respect when you empower people to be creative and resourceful.

Give Credit Where Credit Is Due

Your willingness to recognize people for their contributions shows generosity, fairness, and respect. Sometimes, what people have produced will not be what you expected and will not meet your standards. In those cases, you should still appreciate and recognize what went into completing that work, regardless of its merit, and then find a motivating, constructive way to give feedback and coaching.

Whether things go well or poorly people generally know who's responsible. As the leader or manager of the group, you should accept responsibility if you are at fault. Doing so shows self-esteem and models the behavior you'd like to see from others. When you make mistakes, acknowledge them frankly and forthrightly. If something goes wrong and you're not to blame, try to understand what happened and why, fix the problem, and then use it as an opportunity for individual or group learning. Blaming as a form of punishment is not productive, and it makes people wary of you.

On the other hand, when things go well, share the credit with others, even if you are solely responsible for the success. It's usually true that you couldn't have done it without others' help, even indirect help. Moreover, it makes you magnanimous, and people will want to associate with you because they know that you are generous with praise and aren't trying to grab all the glory yourself.

The research on what people want shows that women and people in their twenties have significantly greater needs for rewards and recognition from their manager and for feeling that their manager values them.

So, although it's important to give credit where credit is due, regardless of the employee, it is especially important for the women and younger people working for you.

Keep Others' Best Interests in Mind

Do you have an inner circle? Favorites among your staff? You probably do. There will always be stars—the people who are more highly skilled, more capable, more intelligent, more resourceful, more professional, more responsive, easier to get along with, and so on. It's easy to favor them because they do so much more for you and are a better match temperamentally. You come to rely on them more, and they become your closest advisers. You give them the most desirable assignments (because you are more confident of them), and they get the lion's share of the rewards, promotions, bonuses, and recognition. Soon you have an inner circle and an outer circle, and those in the outer circle will perceive that the inner-circle people get preferential treatment (which will probably be true) and that the rules that apply to everyone else don't always apply to them (which will probably also be true).

I'm not arguing that you shouldn't have an inner circle. Human nature being what it is, you probably can't avoid having favorites among your staff. Still, you can behave impartially and fairly toward everyone, and you can ensure that you take everyone's best interests to heart. You can ensure that assignments are given fairly, that everyone is recognized for their contributions, and that you give opportunities across the board, regardless of someone's position in the "caste system" in your group. You can also be sure to avoid nepotism or anything else that smacks of favoritism.

Finally, don't give yourself more than your fair share of rewards and benefits. The people who work for you will know how much you've contributed and how central you are to the business. If you take more than what they perceive to be your share of the rewards, they will resent it and will eventually resent you. Many people in the working world suspect that managers and executives take more than their fair share, and the recent scandals at Enron, WorldCom, HealthSouth, and Adelphia, among others, have proved the point. You don't have employees' or shareholders' best interests at heart when you're padding your own pockets.

Go the Extra Mile

I learned a powerful lesson in leadership as a second lieutenant during the Vietnam War. I was leading an ambush patrol through a jungle on a dark night, and we came upon a clearing about fifty feet across. You could see the dense trees on the other side, but it was too dark to see anything in there. My point man knew it was a perfect place to be ambushed, so he stopped when he reached the edge of the clearing. After a moment, I went up and asked why he hadn't crossed the clearing. He said he hadn't seen or heard anything in the trees on the other side but was afraid to go across. He had a sixth sense about it, he said. It felt too dangerous, and he would not budge.

We had to get across that clearing to reach our objective, and I knew at that moment that I had to cross the clearing first. If I didn't, I would lose his respect and the respect of the other soldiers with me. It was one of the key leadership moments in my life. I was aware of the risks, too, and did not feel good about crossing that clearing. Sometimes, someone's sixth sense about danger is contagious, and I wondered if he had seen or heard something on the edge of his awareness. Maybe the enemy was hiding in the trees on the other side. I started to have doubts myself about going across. But it didn't matter. I couldn't ask him to do what I was not willing to do myself. So I walked across the clearing and into the trees and brush on the other side. Nothing happened, so I walked back across and asked him to follow me, and he did.

When things get tough, you have to be willing to lead the way. You have to pitch in. This doesn't mean that if you manage a hotel, for instance, you have to make up the rooms now and then. But if there's a crisis and beds need to be made, then you'd better be willing to go make them. In small, rapidly growing companies, people sometimes expect the company's senior managers to keep doing the hands-on work they've always done, but as the company grows, senior management roles change, and senior managers no longer have the time to do the hands-on work. In fact, as a senior manager, at some point you have to step back totally, because otherwise you meddle in the work your subordinate managers should be doing. Nonetheless, when a crisis occurs, you must be there with your sleeves rolled up. People will trust you when you show that you are willing to get in there with them and get your hands dirty.

Back People Up

Years ago I worked with one manager, Bob, who ran for the hills whenever something went wrong. On one particular project, his team did what they thought was right, but they butted heads with people from another department whose manager complained about it. Rather than gather the facts and support his team (which turned out to have done the right thing), Bob assumed that they were wrong and failed to back them up in the meeting of senior management when the issue was discussed. Moreover, he did not apologize later when his team turned out to have done the right thing. To the people working for you, this kind of behavior is inexcusable and destroys trust faster than anything else other than outright lying and dishonesty.

In another case, a financial manager, Linda, had a group of accountants working for her. When some midlevel line managers violated company policies and wanted the rules bent, the accountants said no. Those managers went around them and appealed directly to Linda, who relented and said yes—and then failed to tell the accountants about her decision or the rationale for it. They later discovered what she'd done when those line managers expected the same exclusions from policy. Naturally the accountants felt betrayed, undermined, and confused, and some of them subsequently resigned and found jobs elsewhere.

You have to support your people when they are doing what they are supposed to be doing. If you think an exception is warranted, talk to them and explain why. Allow them to participate in the decision and help them understand whether they should have done anything differently. It's best to jointly create guidelines where such exceptions should be applied in the future. That way you engage your people in "rule formation" and help them retain the dignity involved in being able to make informed decisions without their bosses' constant oversight and approval.

To a great extent, you should be the protector and defender of your teams. Of course, you don't want to go to extremes and have a "my team right or wrong" attitude. When a team is clearly wrong, you need to let the members know that. It's best to say that although you can't support this decision or solution for the reasons you give them, you still believe in them and support them. People don't expect to have a superhero covering their every move. But they do expect to have a reasonable degree of protection from unwarranted criticism or interference and from corporate politics.

Show Good Judgment

If you are my boss, do you know when to push me harder and when not to? When to ask me about something personal and when not to? Do you know whether I'm sensitive about feedback and coaching and how best to give me feedback? Do you know what I value, what I like, and what I need? Do you know how I like to be recognized and rewarded for my accomplishments? When to examine my work closely and when to trust my work products? To be trustworthy, you need to be able to make judgments like these, to have good interpersonal judgment.

In my experience, good interpersonal judgment is difficult to master because people are different and you can err in being too sensitive, too warm, and too engaging with some people and in being too insensitive, too distant, and too hands-off with others. The trick in interpersonal judgment is to be sensitive to what each person responds to best, what each person likes and prefers, what is important to each person, and so on. Everyone's individual differences must matter to you, and you can't be so busy that you don't attend to those differences. People will find you worthy of trust if they know that you are sensitive to their individual differences and respect those differences in how you behave toward them.

Be a Good Person

Carl Icahn said that if you need a friend, get a dog. You don't have to be a warm and fuzzy person to succeed in business. Martha Stewart is known as a tough businesswoman who is often harsh with staff members and difficult to get along with. Bill Gates has thrown temper tantrums that are legendary. Leona Helmsley, known as the "Queen of Mean," was notably nasty with the people who worked for her and once was reputed to have said that "only the little people pay taxes" (she did jail time for following that tip). I don't want to appear naive in suggesting that to have excellent relationships with employees you have to be a nice person—although it certainly helps. However, if you want people to trust you, you have to be viewed as a good person.

Be Fair

Good people are fair. They treat others with equanimity and respect. They don't joke about people or belittle them behind their backs or engage in destructive gossip. They aren't petty or mean in their dealings with others. They don't try to take advantage and don't demonstrate contempt for others. I once worked with a consultant who had little regard for other people. During one memorably disgusting dinner with him, he rated the husbands or wives of various mutual business acquaintances on a 1 to 10 scale and called some of them dogs or pigs. I wondered at the time how he rated me and my spouse and what he said about us when we were out of earshot. Fortunately, I didn't have to work with him much longer.

If you are arrogant, mean, petty, abrasive, or caustic, and if you show little positive regard for other people through your behavior, jokes, comments, or attitude, people will find you untrustworthy. They may still work with you, but they will be guarded and suspicious. On the other hand, if you have a good heart and a generous spirit, if you treat people with kindness and consideration, you will build trust simply because of your benevolence, and that will open many doors for you.

Maintain Confidences

In my thirty years in business, I've been surprised at how often someone tells me something in confidence. I've been surprised, too, at the number of managers I've met who accepted confidences and then, in the spirit of "knowledge is power," shared those confidences with others as a way of bartering for influence or power. Clearly, people will learn to distrust you if you reveal something you've expressly promised you would keep secret.

Of course, when someone asks you to keep something in confidence, you don't know whether you really can do that until they tell you what it is. If they reveal that they or someone else is doing something illegal or unethical, then you would be complicit if you kept that information confidential. I've found it best to draw a clear line about maintaining confidences. I will keep anything of a personal nature confidential unless you tell me that you are about to harm someone or do something else that is clearly illegal. If it relates to the business and will affect the business, then I have to be able to use my own judgment about what is confidential and what isn't. Moreover, if I believe that something you've told me in confidence should not remain confidential, then I will tell you why and see if we can agree on how and when and by whom the information can be disclosed. But I won't decide on my own to reveal it without consulting with you first.

People have different thresholds of sensitivity on confidential information. If you tell me, for instance, that your spouse is having a medical procedure and you don't explicitly ask me to keep that information private, I have to know whether you would consider that information sensitive and private or not. Would it be acceptable for me to pass on that information to mutual friends? Some people would be grateful if you passed it on; others would be offended. You have to know people well enough to know where their sensitivity lies. Don't assume that because it wouldn't offend you, it wouldn't offend them. If you don't know, ask for permission first, rather than forgiveness later. You may get grudging forgiveness but not without some loss of trust.

How you handle personal, private, or confidential information is one of the foundations of character. Under the precept that knowledge is power, some people treat private information as a tool for gaining and using influence, and some readers would consider my perspective naive. Certainly, it is possible to be Machiavellian in your handling of information others consider confidential, but you are likely to destroy others' trust in you. In the research, more than 85 percent of those surveyed said that their manager's discreet handling of sensitive information was highly important to them.

Be Genuine

I once counseled a woman who complained that her boss, Tom, was like Dr. Jekyll and Mr. Hyde—and she couldn't tell which was the real personality. "I could work for Mr. Hyde," she told me. "As abrasive as he is, at least I'd know what to expect. But most of the time Tom comes across like Dr. Jekyll—kind and considerate, a genuinely nice guy. Then his evil twin emerges, and he's hell on wheels. I'm not sure which one is the real Tom, the beast who knows how to act nice most of the time or the nice guy who eats nails for breakfast."

Unless you're an actor, you can't pretend to be someone you're not—and maintain that facade for very long. The real you, if there is one, is bound to emerge sooner or later, and people will not trust you if they can't figure out which personality is the real you. Sadly, some people do not have an authentic self. In childhood, they never adequately separated from their mother, never developed an authentic self, so they live their lives like chameleons—their sense of self shifting as they interact with other people and try to figure out and adapt to what they think other people want or expect. Clearly, you can be genuine only if there is a genuine you—a fully differentiated, mature adult. Otherwise, your self will shift as the wind shifts, and you will be seen as inconsistent, mercurial, unpredictable, and enigmatic to the people working with you.

That's why people tend to distrust managers who are moody and unpredictable, even if those managers are otherwise excellent and trustworthy. In my coaching work, I've heard comments like the following:

"I'm never sure how he's going to respond." "In meetings you're never sure whether she's going to be terrific or a terror." "We can never tell which side of her is going to show up at work each day." We all get up on the wrong side of the bed now and then, but if you're in a management role you have to be careful about being moody and unpredictable around employees.

Allow Your Humanity to Show

One of my good friends, Paul Krauss, who is a former director at a management consulting firm, often talks about the value of allowing your humanity to show. He tells the story of a young consultant who was setting up an overhead projector in a room full of clients and cut his finger while trying to change the light bulb. Noticing that his finger was bleeding, one of the clients remarked, "My God, they bleed."

We all bleed. We all spill food on our clothing now and then. We make mistakes. We have problems in our personal lives. We get indigestion. When you disclose your foibles, admit your mistakes, and laugh at yourself for being so stupid about something, you show your humanity (and show a huge amount of self-confidence). Moreover, you reveal a side of yourself that others may find endearing because it reminds them of their own humanity. And that's a wonderful way to build trust.

Tips for Improving Your Relationships

1. Be unconditionally honest.

2. Be credible.

3. Keep your commitments.

4. Own up to your mistakes.

5. Care about people.

6. Be available for people when they need you.

7. Be in the moment with people when they are distressed.

8. Don't avoid dealing with people's personal issues.

9. Respect people's work.

10. Give credit where credit is due.

11. Keep others' best interests in mind.

12. Go the extra mile.

13. Back people up.

14. Show good judgment.

15. Be a good person.

16. Be fair.

17. Maintain confidences.

18. Be genuine.

19. Allow your humanity to show.

3 | Setting the Right Tone

S ome years ago I observed two managers whose different interpersonal styles created stark contrasts in the working environments of the groups they managed in the trading company where they worked. Alice had risen through the ranks and had achieved a comfortable level of success. She now sat in her office most of the time and had little day-to-day contact with the traders, who considered her aloof. She would frequently come into and leave the office without speaking to anyone but her assistant. When she did talk to people she rarely smiled, and she had the odd habit of looking away from them while she spoke. When people asked her questions, she would occasionally go off on tangents and answer with something that had little to do with what she was asked.

In contrast, Bill hated sitting in his office. He spent much of his day on the trading floor or out seeing customers. Bill acted like an ex-Marine but in fact had an accounting degree from an Ivy League university and had never served in the military. Among the traders, he was known as a good ole boy. He told jokes, slapped people's backs, and sometimes threw wads of paper across the room to get someone's attention. He had an infectious laugh and a carefree manner, but he also cursed and was sometimes so gruff and crude that he offended even his fellow good ole boys on the trading floor (not to mention offending everyone else).

For very different reasons, neither of these managers was effective at building strong relationships with all the members of their team. However, they taught me an important lesson about interpersonal skills, namely, that a manager's day-to-day behavior with employees sets the tone for the relationship—not a startling realization at first glance, but more profound than it initially appears. Your behavior is rooted in your sense of yourself, in your attitudes toward your work and your employees, in your operating style, in your experience, and in your character. You are how you behave, and your behavior shapes the way people interact with you, accept your direction, listen to your advice, respond to your leadership, communicate with you, and talk about you to others. The tone of the relationship is fundamentally important, and it is created with the simplest behaviors repeated day after day.

Some of these behaviors are so fundamental I'd be embarrassed to discuss them had I not seen thousands of managers who don't do these fundamental things and don't seem to understand why these behaviors are important. A manager such as Alice should understand that her aloofness and distance were having a significantly negative effect on the people she was responsible for. When she looked away while people were speaking to her, she gave the impression that she was distracted, didn't care about them, and disagreed with what they were saying. Her tangential remarks left people feeling that she was in her own world (not a bad assumption to make!) and was losing touch with the day-to-day operations of the business. Because she rarely smiled, people assumed she was depressed, unhappy, or simply bland, and they felt very little connection with her beyond the unfortunate fact that she was their boss.

Bill had far stronger and more personal connections, at least with many of the traders. But he did signal that if you weren't a good ole boy like him you weren't in his inner circle, and he assumed that everyone would enjoy the same off-color jokes he did, which of course was not true, so he came across as an insensitive lout. People tolerated him but were wary, and some people felt that he would not treat them fairly because they weren't cut from his mold and didn't share his sense of humor. The result was a fragmented workforce with a moderate undercurrent of discontent and some serious detractors who passively resisted Bill's efforts. Bill thought he was creating a dynamic team atmosphere with his jovial manner and just-one-of-the-guys attitude, but what he had instead were a handful of buddies and a fractious atmosphere where people acted essentially for themselves and not for the team.

When it comes to behavior, you reap what you sow. If you set the right tone in your relationships with employees, you are likely to get a positive, committed group of people acting in concert to achieve the group's goals.

Here are some commonsense ways to set the right tone.

Smile and Act Friendly

Television's famed Mr. Rogers—who had a warm smile and was perhaps the friendliest human being who ever lived—had a fulfilling life, was loved by millions, and died a wealthy man. We should all be so fortunate.

I'm not suggesting that you put on a happy face and become known for your grin and your cardigan sweater. But one of the strongest, most powerful nonverbal connections you can make with anyone is to smile at them—a brief smile upon greeting, a simple smile in return for a compliment or gesture, a smile to acknowledge something they've said or done, and so on. Smiles work extremely well as relationship builders because smiling can be contagious. When we smile at people, we show a friendly disposition, and they tend to smile back. Obviously, this varies from culture to culture, but we shouldn't make too many assumptions about that. I've found that most people are friendly, especially once the ice has been broken and they are comfortable with you. At work, you should certainly have relationships where smiles will be honored and returned. And here's the real lesson for managers: you smile first. Set the tone by smiling and being friendly with people rather than, like Alice, being withdrawn and aloof.

Wave First and Wave Back

Like smiling, waving at people when you see them is a good icebreaker and requires little effort. Waving is more than a nonverbal greeting. It's a symbol of your approachability, a sign that you've seen and acknowledge the other person, and a ritual form of bonding.

Managers are at both ends of the spectrum on waving and handshaking. Some are too effusive, waving enthusiastically at everyone, slapping people on the back, and pumping people's arms when they shake hands while others are the stick-in-the-muds who don't wave, barely acknowledge anyone else's presence, and give only perfunctory handshakes. The sensible middle-of-the-road approach is to have a friendly disposition toward people; to wave when you see someone from a distance; to wave first and, when someone else waves at you first, to wave back; and to shake people's hands when appropriate with a firm but not crushing grip.

Accentuate the Positive

During his first campaign for the presidency, Bill Clinton's theme was "A Place Called Hope" (he was born in Hope, Arkansas), and his campaign theme song was Fleetwood Mac's "Don't Stop (Thinking about Tomorrow)." Clinton and his campaign managers understood the value of accentuating the positive, and Clinton beat the incumbent president by a wide margin. It's easy to be cynical about campaign rhetoric, but Clinton was, by nature, an optimistic person, and he loved people. As a skilled politician, he knew the value of making people feel good, but being hopeful was genuinely a part of his character, and hope was what the electorate wanted during that presidential campaign.

George H. W. Bush, the president Clinton defeated, was a far more somber man whose demeanor and campaign speeches radiated "realism" rather than hope. I've known managers like Bush who believed in "telling it like it is," in being blunt about what was wrong or what had to be fixed. In meetings, they invariably begin with a discussion of problems, and during performance reviews they focus on the negatives more than the positives. Negativity saps the spirit. It strips hope from the picture and gives people a grim sense of what's in store for them. Who would willingly follow someone who makes them feel like that?

As a rule of thumb, you should state the positives about four times as often as you state the negatives. Ask your staff how you're doing. Do you tend to focus on what's wrong or what's right? Do you create a hopeful atmosphere or one filled with anxiety and dread? Few people in the workplace want a manager who is stupidly optimistic, who is blinded by his own hopefulness and can't see real obstacles in the way, who trumpets all the positives even when people know there are problems. What people want is someone who is optimistic and positive by nature but who is realistic enough to see the challenges and pitfalls ahead—and then to plan and work to avoid them.

Lead and Close with What You Like

Occasionally, you have to give people corrective feedback or conduct a performance review and identify areas where people need to improve.

I've seen the full spectrum of approaches to this challenge—from managers who couldn't bring themselves to be direct about the problems they observed to those who focused only on the negatives and never gave any positive reinforcement. Clearly, neither of these extremes works.

When you have to give people corrective feedback or conduct a performance review, lead and close with what you like about a person and his or her performance. Identify problem areas, then have the courage to be direct and compassionate about them, but always try to lead and close by identifying what you like. It's easier for people to accept criticism or negative feedback if you have couched it in positives and given them hopeful messages as well as corrective ones. Having said that, when someone does something seriously wrong, it can seem disingenuous if you lead with a positive comment. They usually know they did something terribly wrong, so it's best to get right to the point, discuss it sensitively but directly, and then close with an affirmative message if you can.

Don't Be Cynical or Sarcastic

Of all the cynical managers I've known, Emily stands out. In charge of a technology development group in a medium-sized Silicon Valley firm, she was considered a brilliant raconteur. She could be witty and charming, but her comments and observations were often laced with acid. Irreverent and sometimes bawdy, she put down anyone and everyone. Although people enjoyed listening to her, they found her hard to take in large doses, and she eventually left the company because she was not being promoted and felt she was in a rut. The real reason may have been her growing realization that few people enjoyed working with her. If you put people down or talk about others behind their backs, people will learn to distrust you because you are likely to talk about them, too, behind their backs.

Cynics make good comedians and newspaper columnists, but they don't necessarily make good leaders. Proud of their own wit and needful of an audience, they often can't curtail their biting remarks, and over time they erode people's estimates of the present and hopes for the future. If you are one of these dazzling wits, consider the impact your sarcasm has on the people you want to follow you and leave the sarcasm and cynicism to late-night television comedians and irreverent newspaper columnists.

Avoid Off-Color or Insensitive Jokes

I've done a lot of work in the engineering and construction industry, where joke telling is considered a fine art and sharing jokes is a form of social bonding. Some clients begin nearly every lunch, dinner, or informal meeting by telling the latest jokes they've heard, and some of these jokes are pretty racy, if not downright tasteless. And, lest you think this is just a male bonding ritual, let me say that some of the best joke tellers I've known have been women. In recent years, joke sharing on the Internet has become the rage. I don't think a day goes by when someone isn't e-mailing me the latest joke.

Joke sharing can be fun, and it is a form of bonding. However—and it's a big *however*—you have to be sensitive to your audience. If you tell jokes or pass them along to people through e-mail, be careful about *who* you share *which* jokes with. Jokes have a kind of feast or famine quality to them—either they work spectacularly well in building relationships or they fail miserably and cause awkwardness, embarrassment, and even anger. Choose your jokes carefully, and tell them only when you are absolutely certain that no one will be offended. If in doubt, don't do it. Furthermore, off-color jokes or jokes that disparage nationalities, races, genders, or religious groups are never okay. They are especially not okay coming from a manager. As a boss, you have to hold yourself to a higher standard of conduct. You should model fairness to all people, a generous and humane spirit, and proper social conduct.

Respect Others' Space

To set the right tone in relationships, you have to respect and preserve people's space—their physical and psychological boundaries. At the physical level, preserving that space means keeping an appropriate distance from people when you approach and stand next to them or sit beside them. It also means not speaking too loudly, not touching them inappropriately, and shaking hands with a comfortable but not too firm grip. At the psychological level, preserving that space means respecting their privacy, not intruding into areas of their lives where you are unwelcome, not imposing your beliefs on them, and giving them the psychological freedom to be themselves.

Most of us grew up with an innate sense of the physical boundaries different people expect us to observe depending on our relationship with them, but I've seen many situations where a person in authority did not grasp this and was threatening or intimidating to people because he or she stood too close, talked too loud, or touched people in ways that made them uncomfortable. You will generally know when you are too close because the other person will look uncomfortable and may back away or otherwise move physically to create more distance between you and him or her. You have to be sensitive to these cues and adjust your distance accordingly.

Similarly, you have to be sensitive about how much you look people in the eye. When people are uncomfortable with prolonged eye contact, they will generally look away from you, and that is your cue to lower the intensity in your eye contact with them.

Respecting someone's physical space also means speaking at a volume that is neither too loud nor too soft and speaking at a comfortable pace. Most of us instinctively vary our volume and pace depending on the situation, the location, the person, and the ambient noise level. However, bullies typically stand too close to people, speak too loudly and rapidly, and intimidate by touching inappropriately, slapping the person's back, or pointing fingers, usually in the other person's face. People who behave like this are usually insecure themselves, and they use intimidation as a way to make themselves feel superior and make others feel inferior or afraid. Bill, whom I talked about at the beginning of this chapter, was one of those. He defended his behavior by claiming to have the best of intentions and thought of himself as just being enthusiastic, but the effect on many of his people was decidedly negative.

Another way to respect people's physical space is to respect how and when they want to be touched—which may mean not at all. Permissible touching has many cultural overtones, but the rule of thumb on touching people, especially employees, is to be highly sensitive to each person's boundaries and preferences—and don't touch them unless it is explicitly okay to do so. It's particularly important for managers to avoid touching members of the opposite sex without permission, and even then it's best to err on the side of caution. The power differential in the manager-employee relationship makes touching employees a highly charged and potentially dangerous area. A hug between colleagues might be okay, but it would not be welcome with the manager. You may have good intentions and intend to be nothing more than friendly, but your intent does not matter. What matters is how employees receive it, and you can't always predict how employees will receive your good intentions. If you are unsure about the boundaries, then don't take the risk.

You need to be cautious about violating not only employees' physical space but also their psychological space. Some managers have been known to spy on employees, going through their desks after hours, reading their mail or e-mails, and otherwise violating their privacy. Obviously, if you suspect someone of theft, industrial espionage, or some other legitimate offense, you need to take steps, but it's best to take action through human resources or security or some other department whose charter includes investigating these kinds of problems.

Respecting people's psychological space also means being careful not to intrude into areas of their lives where you are unwelcome. A woman I interviewed said her manager asked about her pending divorce. A very private person, she did not want to say anything but worried that he might think she was being uncooperative if she refused to say anything. She did tell him about it, and he kept asking for more and more details. When I asked him about it, he thought he was just being sympathetic with an employee's personal problems. He had no clue that she felt victimized by his probing.

Finally, you violate people's psychological space when you appear to be imposing your views on them. The United States Air Force Academy was once criticized, for instance, because some of its highest-ranking officers and influential senior cadets were openly espousing Christian fundamentalist views, and many cadets who didn't share those views felt pressured to convert to avoid being ostracized. In an American institution funded by tax dollars, this behavior is especially reprehensible, but it's dangerous in any organization. Managers with strong religious or political opinions need to be careful not to express their opinions in ways that employees might see as pressure to conform to those views.

It will probably come as no surprise that women are especially concerned about people respecting their space. More than half of the women surveyed said that having their managers and coworkers respect their space was highly important to them. What may be surprising, however, is that women felt even more strongly about their close friends and family respecting their space. More than two-thirds of them rated this as highly important. Much more so than men, women have a strong need for boundaries—and for others to respect those boundaries.

Respecting their space is also significantly more important to younger employees than it is to older employees. Younger workers are more independent than previous generations. Sixty percent of them rate this as a very strong need. So if you violate, intentionally or otherwise, a younger worker's personal space, you are more likely to lose that person.

Attend to People's Cares and Concerns

While you need to respect people's privacy, you also need to attend to people's cares and concerns—*where your attention is welcome.* John, the manager I talked about in the Introduction, was insensitive in this way. Occasionally, he could see that something was wrong with someone, but he chose to ignore it. When you sense that someone is feeling bad or out of sorts or is otherwise not acting like himself or herself, you should notice. You can test whether they want to talk about it by asking, "Is everything all right?" If the person says no, then say, "Is there any way I can help?" or "Is it something you'd feel comfortable talking about?" If the person is willing to discuss it, then find a private place to talk.

The tone you want to set is one of sensitivity and caring within a professional setting where the work is paramount but where individual issues and concerns are recognized, respected, and dealt with to the extent they can be. People want to know that you care and that you and the organization will do what you can for people when they are in need. Indeed, some companies become renowned for how well they look after their employees, and these companies typically wind up on *Fortune* magazine's "Best Companies to Work For" lists. The more you care about employees and attend to their concerns, the more loyal they are likely to be to the company.

An important caveat about caring is that only a third of employees say they want this from their manager (however, nine out of ten people say they expect caring from their close friends and family). But it's important to distinguish between the kind of deep, personal caring people expect from those close to them and the normal standard of caring they expect from their boss. The majority of employees may not expect their managers to care for them the way their close friends and family do, but they do expect managers to care at some level. In Chapter 4, I have much more to say about managers' levels of caring.

Assume Benign Intent

Unless you have direct evidence that some employee is being dishonest or disruptive, you should assume benign intent. Assume that people are committed, will do the best job they can, will not take undue advantage, care about quality, will go the extra mile when they have to, and will treat you fairly if you treat them fairly. Remember that what people want most is to feel trusted. If you demonstrate trust in them, most will respond with trustworthy behavior.

Still, there are undoubtedly some employees who don't deserve a high level of trust. A few aren't loyal and will never be, take every possible advantage, don't work as hard as they could, don't care about quality, aren't willing to put forth the extra effort when it's needed, play every angle, and so on. The best thing you can do for you and them is to boot them out as quickly as possible. They poison the well.

Make People Feel Important

Self-esteem is a powerful driver for people. People want to feel that they matter, that their contributions are important to the organization, that they have value as human beings. Everyone wants to feel important.

The most obvious ways to help people feel good about themselves are to give them meaningful work to do, give them more responsibility, ask them to represent the group to outsiders, ask them to participate on special teams or task forces, and recognize them publicly for their accomplishments. In short, make them feel important by having them do things they know are important and give them a lot of visibility in their role. However, there are more fundamental ways to make people feel important.

- Remember people's names. If you don't remember someone's name, that person isn't important to you. Better yet, remember some facts about their life and mention those facts from time to time. Showing interest in someone as a person—not just as an employee—signifies that you consider that person important.

- Pay attention to people by acknowledging their presence. When you pass someone in the hallway, make eye contact, nod or say hello, or stop to chat for a moment. I've seen senior executives walk down a long hallway full of employees and act as if none of them were there. It's a demeaning experience for the people who are ignored, and it establishes an imperial tone in the manager-employee relationship.

- Give people time. The more time you give them, the more important they will feel. Of course, you don't have a lot of time, and they will be busy, too. So develop the art of finding the right precious moments to spend with everyone who does matter to you, and give them the one-on-one time with you that indicates that you consider them important.

- Include people in your communications. The best communications are one-on-one in the form of letters, personal e-mails, and individual telephone calls. However, you also signal importance when you include people on e-mail distribution lists. Pay attention to the lists of people you choose to communicate with, and be strategic about including people you want to feel important. At the same time, respect the fact that people are already overwhelmed with e-mail, and don't send people messages that don't really pertain to them.

■ Call upon people's knowledge and expertise. Clearly, you show that you consider people important when you ask for their opinions, call upon their expertise, or rely upon them to accomplish something that matters.

Remember that as the manager your opinion of people is critically important to them. You can make structural decisions that signify importance—like giving someone a new position or a raise—but it's your day-to-day behavior toward people that has the greatest impact on their sense of importance.

When People Are Talking to You, Face Them

I once worked with an executive whose leadership ratings seemed lower than they should have been considering his personality and other attributes. He was smart, capable, and by all appearances a natural leader. But his direct reports complained that he was too distracted and wouldn't give them the time of day. Some thought that he felt he was too good for them.

As I got to know him, I realized that the problem was almost entirely nonverbal. He was busy and would not completely break from what he was doing when someone came into his office to talk. He was good enough at multitasking that he could be in a conversation with someone while reading e-mails or working on his laptop or doing something else. I was amazed that he seemed to be able to do two different things at once, but he could—and he could remember what happened in both. But the net effect, of course, was that when people spoke to him he seemed distracted and indifferent. The simple suggestion that he stop multitasking and face the person talking to him turned the negative impressions around right away.

Your body language has tremendous impact on the impression you create with people. If you appear distracted or bored, they assume you aren't interested in them or what they are saying. When they speak to you, set the right tone by facing them and giving them your full attention.

When People Are Talking to You, Minimize Distractions

When you're talking to someone, avoid looking out the window, glancing at your desk, reading a document, checking your e-mail, taking phone calls, or thumbing through your Blackberry. I used to be one of those people who are addicted to their Blackberrys. When my Blackberry buzzed, I felt compelled to check it. I'm recovering now and am learning to turn it off when I'm someplace where I shouldn't be distracted and not to have a knee-jerk reaction when an e-mail message arrives, especially if I'm talking to someone. When you are with people, *really* be with them. Put your phone on Do Not Disturb or don't answer calls. Turn off your Blackberry or ignore it. Being fully present with someone shows respect and signals that that person is important to you.

You want to set a tone that is respectful and friendly—one that establishes a foundation of trust, cooperation, enthusiasm, and commitment. Obviously, you want to avoid antagonism, distrust, compliance (rather than commitment), lethargy, and indifference.

The people who work for you are more likely to be dedicated and productive if you are warm and friendly (as opposed to being cold and distant), if you are positive and hopeful (as opposed to being cynical and sarcastic), if you are respectful of their need for privacy and you demonstrate trust, if you pay attention to them and show that you care about them as individuals, if you make them feel important, and if you give them your undivided attention when they are speaking to you. When you are already overwhelmed by the demands on your time, it's difficult to give everyone the time they would like, so you may have to set aside time to be fully present with people.

Building and maintaining healthy work relationships is not easy, especially in a world where things move at light speed and there are multiple, conflicting, high-priority demands on your time. However, the work your organization needs to do—and do efficiently and pro-ductively—can be done only by the people you manage (and the people they manage). The way you treat your people has a tremendous impact on their attitudes, their productivity, their commitment to you and the organization, and their behavior toward your customers or clients.

Obviously, there will be times when employees disappoint you, when they are lax or careless, when they treat someone badly, and when you need to be tough and correct behavior that is having a negative effect on your clients or customers or your team. Even in those circum-stances, you should treat those employees with sensitivity and respect. I know that can be difficult. I've been in those situations myself, and sometimes you want to go into a dark room by yourself and scream at the walls before you confront the problem employee. Sometimes your own anger is palpable and it is best to discharge it or let things cool off before you talk to the person causing the problem. Yelling at an employee or expressing your anger publicly is never a good idea. It can make you look petty, immature, and spiteful. It rocks everyone back on their heels. And it creates a tense atmosphere that infects everyone's spirits. (See Chapter 8 for more on keeping an even keel.)

The best you can do in all circumstances is to be graceful in your behavior toward all people but especially toward those you manage. Your role as manager gives you an inordinate amount of influence over their lives, so you bear an inordinate amount of responsibility for how you treat them. I think Anne Morrow Lindbergh said it best in her book *Gift from the Sea:* "I want first of all . . . to be at peace with myself. I want a singleness of eye, a purity of intention, a central core to my life that will enable me to carry out these obligations and activities as well as I can. I want, in fact . . . to live 'in grace' as much of the time as possible."[1]

The tone you establish in your relationships with other people reflects your inner self. If you are at peace with yourself and feel the inner harmony Lindbergh speaks of, you are likely to behave gracefully toward other people—and this is the key to setting a warm and positive tone in your working relationships.

Tips for Improving Your Relationships

1. Smile and act friendly.

2. Wave first and wave back.

3. Accentuate the positive.

4. Lead and close with what you like.

5. Don't be cynical or sarcastic.

6. Avoid off-color or insensitive jokes.

7. Respect others' space.

8. Attend to people's cares and concerns.

9. Assume benign intent.

10. Make people feel important.

11. When people are talking to you, face them.

12. When people are talking to you, minimize distractions.

4 | Being Sensitive

People who have superior human relations skills are highly sensitive to others' feelings. They sense when things are going well or poorly for someone—and they respond to their perceptions by showing that they care. They also know and care about how they are coming across with people, what impact they are having. They sense people's moods, share in their joys, and commiserate with their troubles. They care if someone is hurt, wounded, or feeling frustrated; conversely, they share someone's feelings of excitement, joy, or playfulness. In short, these people are highly empathetic.

We sometimes believe, stereotypically, that women are more empathetic than men and have better people skills, but my experience does not bear this out. I've met scores of women who are insensitive, incapable of dealing with people, and even spiteful or cruel in their treatment of others, and I've met hundreds of men who are highly sensitive, care about other people, and are skilled at interacting with others. Sensitivity is not gender based. It is a quality of character and spirit that enables those who are highly sensitive to display a degree of empathy and caring that attracts other people, instills trust, and builds strong bonds.

Can Sensitivity Be Learned?

Experts are still trying to reach a consensus on when, where, and how we acquire empathy. Recent studies suggest that human beings are prewired to be empathetic, at least to a certain degree. While the depth and sophistication of empathy is deemed a developmental virtue, experts such as Diane Montague of La Salle University, Charles Nelson of Harvard, and Martin Hoffman of New York University believe the foundation already exists. According to Montague's studies, babies younger than six months are capable of understanding the emotions behind different facial expressions and responding in kind. Other studies involved exposing infants to the sounds of their own cries and the cries of other infants. The sounds of their own cries did not significantly affect them, but when they heard other infant cries they immediately started crying themselves.[1] For the most part, however, empathy and sensitivity to others seem to be a learned set of attitudes and behaviors, the product of conditioning as we develop through childhood.

Although some people who are insensitive toward others—including some with narcissistic traits—are probably psychopaths who behave the way they do because of brain chemistry, the vast majority of people can't use faulty brain chemistry as an excuse. My experience in coaching hundreds of managers whom others described as abrasive, insensitive, or uncaring is that most were capable of learning new behaviors once they understood and fully appreciated the negative impact their behavior had on other people. Still, you can't turn a boor into a model of thoughtfulness, and some people will continue to be insensitive and uncaring no matter how many times they get feedback and coaching about it. The plain fact is that these people know they're doing harm and don't care. This book is not for them.

However, most people do care if they are being insensitive. They are often just oblivious to other people because they have other things on their mind, like the engineer who is so focused on the problem he's solving that he doesn't sense what's happening with the people around him. Or the finance manager whose mind is so totally absorbed by the numbers and details of her job that she's unaware when someone is upset— or she's aware but doesn't think it's any of her business, or she knows something is wrong but is uncomfortable dealing with it because she's not sure what to do or say. But if you point out to these people that they are being insensitive, most of them will feel bad about that. Sometimes people simply aren't aware of the impact of their insensitivity on others or don't appreciate how much damage they are doing.

Being More Sensitive

I think you can learn to modify your behavior if you actually care about the impact you are having on others. Having said that, let me add that if you manage other people, you darn well should care. Even if you have an engineering background and love technical problem solving, or if you're a finance whiz and love numbers, when you manage other people you are obliged by the role you play to be sensitive, care about them, and care about the impact of your behavior.

Being more sensitive to people means connecting with your heart as well as your head. Here are some ways you can do that.

Behave Gracefully toward Other People

At the end of the last chapter, I introduced the concept of grace. Anne Morrow Lindbergh defined grace as "an inner harmony, essentially spiritual, which can be translated into outward harmony." We project to the outside world what is within. Grace, especially in human relations, begins with inner harmony, with a contentedness and peacefulness within yourself. It is difficult to wrestle with internal demons, to experience strife at the core of your being, and at the same time behave gracefully toward others. Too often, the raw turmoil within surfaces in your treatment of others. But if you experience inner harmony and are at peace with yourself, the way is clear for you to behave graciously and compassionately toward others. Why? Perhaps because you have nothing to prove to yourself, no hidden demons to fight, and, being more accepting of your own humanity, are more willing to accept the humanity of others. The foundation of sensitivity is just that—the recognition and acceptance of others' humanity.

Of course, I recognize how difficult it can be to achieve that inner harmony. People approach it through self-study, reading, education, religion, spirituality, therapy, work, art, relationships, and other paths— and many people remain on this quest for a lifetime. Perhaps it is *the* lifetime journey for most of us, and perhaps we never resolve it fully, never reach nirvana. Still, many people are able to achieve a state of peace within themselves, a contentedness that springs from healthy self-acceptance and a mature and healthy ego, that enables them to relate to others in a graceful way. Others can never quiet the restless demons within, and those demons emerge in a callousness toward others, or in inappropriate anger toward an employee who got something wrong, or in insensitivity toward a coworker who has a personal problem that is interfering with his or her work.

It helps, frankly, if you have experienced, on the one hand, pain and inner turmoil yourself, and, on the other, the triumph and joy of success. Undergoing the suffering and joy that other people experience increases your empathy toward them. This is why psychotherapists who've had no struggles themselves make the worst therapists and why actors who've led charmed lives make the worst actors. Psychotherapy is empathy practiced in psychological healing; acting is empathy projected onto the stage. Both require the practitioner to have undergone the experiences that make others both human and flawed.

So grace derives in part from a sense of commonality with other people, with the capacity to see their experiences as your own. That doesn't mean that you have to have exact or even similar experiences. You can empathize with a grieving mother whose son or daughter was killed in Iraq even if you aren't a mother and haven't lost a child because you know or can imagine what it would be like to lose someone very precious. You can empathize with an employee whose wife has been diagnosed with breast cancer because at some point in your life you have experienced fear and foreboding yourself. And you can empathize with an employee who just received an award for community service because you know what it feels like to be congratulated, applauded, or recognized publicly. Empathy means to feel what the other person feels, to put yourself emotionally in that person's place. It is one of the deepest connections we can have with other people who are not related to us by blood because we connect with them at the emotional level. It's a *heart* connection rather than a *head* connection.

Some years ago I was hiking in southern Utah in an area the Anasazi people had inhabited a thousand years ago. These were the Native Americans who built the cliff dwellings at Mesa Verde and Chaco Canyon and who left cliff paintings all over the desert Southwest. I was hiking over a long stretch of sandstone hills and saw dark cumulus clouds forming over the mountains nearby. The clouds were rolling in quickly, and I knew that a late afternoon thunderstorm would soon occur. I was in an exposed area, so I looked for shelter. In the distance, I saw a large overhang, a great prow of rock with a deep shadow beneath it, not a cave but a place so recessed that it would provide ample shelter. I picked up my pace and made it to the overhang just as the rain began.

Sitting under the rock while the storm pounded the ground outside, I realized that this place was a perfect shelter, not only from thunderstorms but from the wind and the baking sun on long summer days. It was the only place within eyesight that afforded this kind of shelter. The

Anasazis who walked and hunted here a thousand years ago would have known that. They would have sought shelter under this same overhang. They would have been sitting where I was, watching the storm, waiting for it to pass. I am not of their tribe, and I was separated from them by a thousand years, but at that moment, during that storm, I felt a deep sense of connectedness with those people because of our common experience under that perfect shelter in the vast desert and sandstone hills of what is now southern Utah.

The capacity to see others' experiences as your own and to feel a sense of connectedness with them despite differences in time or space, race, religion, or ethnicity enables you to be more understanding of people and more forgiving of their idiosyncrasies, occasional mistakes or misfires, and common human failings. Moreover, that capacity stems the tendency to be prideful and arrogant. It's hard to feel a sense of commonality with people and feel superior to them at the same time. The narcissists who behave dismissively toward those who fail to meet their high standards invariably believe that they are not like other people, that they are *special* in some way, and it is *that* disconnectedness from others that generally fuels arrogant and condescending behavior.

The managers I've known who were models of graceful behavior kept a healthy perspective about themselves and the people they managed. Although they were recognized for their leadership skills and promoted into positions of greater authority and responsibility, they did not let it go to their head. They knew that fundamentally they were no different from the people who reported to them. That sense of perspective kept them humble, which is one of the characteristics of Jim Collins's Level 5 leaders, those who led "every good-to-great company . . . during the pivotal transition years." These leaders "display workman-like diligence" and are "fanatically driven, infected with an incurable need to produce sustained results"; they also display "a compelling modesty" and "are self-effacing and understated," unlike the "leaders with gargantuan personal egos that contributed to the demise or continued mediocrity" of their low-performing companies.[2]

Graceful behavior in managers is not a "touchy feely" concept divorced from business reality. The great companies that Jim Collins studied were led by business leaders who were modest and self-effacing rather than grandiose, arrogant, egotistical, abrasive, and callous toward others. This is not to say that scoundrels don't prevail now and then, but Collins's research shows that *sustained success* is not achieved by swashbucklers with rampant egos and a trail of broken bodies in their wake. On the contrary, sustained superior performance comes from leaders who are modest but still driven to achieve results, sensitive *and* workmanlike, considerate *and* diligent—leaders who understand that sustained business success requires a committed workforce of people who feel good about what they are doing, where they are working, and whom they are working for.

Be Sensitive to Deviations from the Norm

When you work with people long enough, you get to know their moods, attitudes, and demeanors well enough to pick up signs when something is different—and the prerequisite for being more sensitive to people is being sensitive to these deviations from the norm. The signs are often subtle: someone who normally makes eye contact in meetings doesn't, someone who normally smiles when passing you in the hallway looks distracted, someone whose voice is normally pleasant sounds stressed, someone who returns messages quickly fails to respond, someone who is normally decisive isn't, someone who is normally talkative and has good ideas becomes less talkative and doesn't contribute creatively, and so on. When someone's normal pattern of behavior changes, it is usually a sign that something has gone wrong or, possibly, that something has gone delightfully right. In either case, the person is behaving differently and you need to notice that.

Once you notice a change, what do you do about it? The answer is not necessarily to respond to every signal you pick up. Being sensitive is good, but being hypersensitive can drive people crazy. Maybe the person just had a bad night's sleep or is worried about something that has nothing to do with the business and is handling work just fine, thank you very much. It's possible to err by being too sensitive to signals that something is different—but the more common error is not noticing these signals or noticing and not responding to the ones you really should respond to. The art in human relations is in knowing when to ask someone if things are okay and when to leave them alone, and this varies by individual. Some people want you to notice if things are not okay; some people prefer to be left alone; some will reach a threshold where it's imperative that you notice—and they'll consider you insensitive if you don't.

The reason people behave differently is often that they are under stress. When people are under stress, their adrenaline starts flowing, their brain invokes the fight-or-flight response to danger, their heart rate and blood pressure increase, and their breathing becomes more shallow. Behaviorally, people under stress often become more focused on what they need to do, they don't listen as well, they talk faster, they're more impatient, and they are often curt and perhaps even abrasive with people they would normally be kind and courteous to. When you see someone under stress, the worst thing to do is tell them to calm down or take it easy—advice that generally makes the situation worse. The best thing to do is step back, avoid taking offense at their behavior (if it is offensive), try to understand the source of stress, and then see what you can do to help.

Finally, at times you may be so focused on an assignment or a business issue that you fail to immediately register when someone has a problem and needs empathy. I've done this a hundred times. You go to someone for a quick answer, you get what you need, and then you go back to your work. After a while, it registers that the person you went to wasn't behaving normally, or seemed mildly distraught, or was unusually cheerful. You notice belatedly that something is different. When that happens, when it registers, you should go back and acknowledge what you observed. It's never too late to empathize.

Distinguish between a Person's Being and His or Her Current Behavior

Some people handle stress relatively well and are able to work through it with minimal visible effects, but others are like Dr. Jekyll and Mr. Hyde—pleasant, professional, focused, and hard working normally but ill-tempered, moody, unfocused, and abrasive while under stress. When you have to deal with an employee who's under stress, you may just want to tell the stressed person to get over it and get on with it. This is rarely an effective coping strategy. The net effect is that you exacerbate whatever's already stressing that person and make things worse. The more effective strategy—even when you just don't have time for it—is to remind yourself to be patient and try to be understanding and supportive, which can be difficult to do when you are also feeling time pressure and stress. Nonetheless, if you're the one in charge, you bear the burden of being calm and helping everyone else get through it.

The worst thing you can do is adopt the attitude that employees' problems are their problems, that they should leave those problems at home, and that anything that gets in the way of their getting the job done is a distraction that can be ignored. When you sense something out of the ordinary, determine, based on your knowledge of each person, whether this deviation from the norm is something you should ask about, something that should be addressed. Show that you've noticed and ask if the person is okay or would like to talk about it. Noticing is the most obvious early sign that you care (the related signs of caring are that you take the issues seriously, that you care about the person's life, that you will do what you can to help, and that you understand and accept that people have problems from time to time). You don't expect them to be robotic and never have things troubling them. They aren't robots. They're people, and you need to show that you sense something's out of sorts and care about that. Mostly, you need to show that you care whether the people who work for you are okay; and if they're not, that you will do what you can to help.

Show Empathy When Others Reveal Their Feelings

I once coached a manager who seemed oblivious to people's feelings. While observing him working with his team, I overheard the following exchange:

> *Employee:* I know this should be done by now, but I just can't figure it out. Something's missing.
>
> *Manager:* Have you called Finance? What did they say?
>
> *Employee:* Yes, three times. I've left messages, but no one's gotten back to me.
>
> *Manager:* We need to get this done today.
>
> *Employee:* I know that, I know. It's frustrating as hell, but I just can't get the data I need.
>
> *Manager:* Then just do a best estimate for now. You can redo it when Finance gets back to you.
>
> *Employee:* I'm not sure I could do even a back-of-the-envelope calculation. I need to know what's in the budget and what's been spent, item by item.

Manager: Well, do the best you can.

Employee: What do you think I've been doing?

This conversation gets derailed from the start and has little hope of reaching a satisfactory conclusion for anyone. The manager is trying to problem-solve, which may or may not be helpful, but the employee's frustration gets in the way of doing that rationally. When people's emotions rule their cognitive processes, they have a hard time being rational. They won't hear rational arguments or process them objectively. The solution is simple: acknowledge the emotions first. Deal with the irrational before trying to be rational. A better dialogue with this employee might go as follows:

Employee: I know this should be done by now, but I just can't figure it out. Something's missing.

Manager: You seem really frustrated. [This response is an example of what psychologist Carl Rogers called "active listening." By hearing the employee's emotions, rather than just the facts, the manager is connecting with the deeper part of the employee's mental state. This is an outstanding example of empathy.]

Employee: Yeah, I am. Frustrated as hell. I've called Finance three times and left messages, and I can't get anyone to return my calls. Meanwhile, I don't have the information I need, and I know we're facing a deadline.

Manager: Well, I understand your frustration. It's aggravating when you're up against a deadline and the people you're relying on for help aren't coming through. [This is another great example of empathy—putting yourself in the other person's shoes and understanding the issues from his or her perspective.]

Employee: Damn right.

Manager: Well, I know how that feels. I've been there. [Empathy and connection.]

Employee: It's not that I don't want to get this done—and quickly.

Manager: I'd want to get it done quickly, too. (pause) So let's think about what it's going to take to get the information you need. What are your options at this point? [Excellent. Go from empathy to problem solving.]

Sometimes, people just need to vent. They need someone else to know how they're feeling. I think this is particularly true of anger and frustration. Those emotions demand an audience. We want people to know that we're frustrated or mad. Once we vent our emotions, we can usually take a step back and look rationally at the alternatives. But whether the emotions are anger, frustration, worry, sadness, fear, or joy, it always helps when someone important to you (and a boss is one of those people) knows what you're feeling and can understand and perhaps even share in your feelings.

Having your feelings acknowledged can be a simple but powerful form of bonding between people, depending on how that acknowledgement occurs. If the person showing empathy does it with a judgment, then it will backfire miserably:

Manager: You seem really frustrated. What's that about? Get a grip, all right? Nobody said this was going to be easy.

It also doesn't help if you're glib about it:

Manager: You seem really frustrated. Don't worry. You'll feel better in the morning. Just go out and have a good stiff drink tonight.

The problem with judgment is that it makes people feel shamed. They are humiliated by being judged, and this lessens their ability to listen actively, recognize what they might do differently, and learn from the experience. It also makes them feel shamed in your presence because they know that you are aware of their frailties and may think less of them as a consequence. To empathize effectively, you need to *recognize* the person's emotional state and then find a sensitive and sensible way to *acknowledge* it. The point is to "be with" the person rather than being objectively outside what the person is feeling. And you should be polite, serious, and kind as you empathize. Avoid wisecracks, silliness, and sarcasm in acknowledging how people feel. People's emotions are usually no laughing matter to them, especially the negative emotions such as fear, anger, and frustration. Always treat those feelings seriously.

Don't Fake Caring

One manager I worked with took pride in reducing people to tears. At the end of a long day with clients, he would insist that his team gather for candid feedback. In grueling sessions that everyone came to dread, he would lay people bare with stinging criticism, which he often delivered with a faint smile. He justified his sadism by saying that he was doing them a favor, that his candor came from an abiding sense of integrity, that he would be dishonest with himself and others if he were not frank in his observations of their performance and their shortcomings. He would occasionally praise someone as well, but the majority of his comments were laced with acid. He was one of the most insensitive human beings I've ever known. And one of the cruelest.

This manager was good at faking caring. He was smart and observant. He had seen leaders who really did care about people and saw how those leaders behaved in their interactions with others. Although he didn't feel any genuine caring himself, he could mimic caring behavior and could be warm and charming when he put on his game face. Over

the period that I watched him interacting with employees and customers, I realized that some people never saw through his facade, but
those who did learned to distrust him—and most eventually did. Over
time, they recognized that his charm and apparent warmth were simply
tools for getting what he wanted, and they felt manipulated and used.

Unless you are a very good actor and are "on stage" all the time, it's
hard to fake caring. Most people are savvy enough to know when you're
being sincere and when you aren't. Most have seen enough phonies in
their lives to recognize phoniness when they experience it, and those
who don't see through fake caring will eventually get it because they'll
talk at the water cooler or in the employee lunchroom to those who do
see through the facade. I have yet to meet a manager who could fake caring and get away with it for very long.

Care for the People Who Work for You

Although you shouldn't try to fake it, caring doesn't necessarily mean
caring deeply about an employee's personal life, family, or career. Caring
is not an all-or-nothing proposition. The table on the following pages
shows the range of things managers might care about, along with the
kinds of behaviors normally associated with each level of caring.

Obviously, the range of caring shown in the table moves from less
personal to more personal. It's hard to imagine any competent manager
who wouldn't care about Levels 1 and 2 (although I've known a few who
didn't), but to be sensitive and caring you don't have to be at Level 7
with everyone who works for you. In all likelihood, your range of caring
varies to some degree by employee—with some you will care deeply
about their personal lives and loved ones; with others you may care
about their health and happiness but not more. To some extent, caring
has to be mutual. If an employee doesn't care about you, it's hard to care

Manager's Levels of Caring for Employees

Level	Focus of Caring	Representative Behaviors
LEVEL 1	**Motivation:** you care that the intrinsic and extrinsic rewards they receive are adequate to keep them engaged and performing well.	• Conduct performance reviews. • Do employee satisfaction surveys. • Ask if they are satisfied. • Give/receive feedback on job performance.
LEVEL 2	**Job satisfaction:** you care that they like their jobs, that what they do is gratifying.	• Note their moods as they work and inquire if someone seems unhappy or bored. • Try to assign people tasks you know they will find gratifying. • Solicit feedback and respond with concern if you pick up signals of dissatisfaction or lack of engagement. • Allow job redefinition if someone is not happy with current responsibilities.
LEVEL 3	**Growth and career:** you care whether they are developing professionally.	• Help them think through their development needs; know how each person needs to grow. • Help employees create individual development plans. • Be an active coach and mentor. • Actively support education and training. • Help them with career planning.

TABLE 1 CONTINUED

Level	Focus of Caring	Representative Behaviors
LEVEL 4	**Health and welfare:** you care about their health and welfare.	• Note when someone doesn't seem to feel well and ask if he or she is okay. • When someone is sick, show concern and insist that they take care of themselves. • Reinforce positive behaviors like quitting smoking, exercising, eating healthful food. • Point them to resources or services to help them with their health where appropriate. • If someone is injured or hospitalized, visit them and do what you can to help.
LEVEL 5	**Emotional state:** you care about their happiness.	• Get to know people's emotional norms and ask when something seems wrong or remarkably different. • If someone is sad, upset, or unhappy express concern and offer to help if you can. • If someone is happy, share the joy. • If someone is angry, be calm, try to understand the issues, commiserate if appropriate, and talk it through.
LEVEL 6	**The people:** you care about their hopes, dreams, and ambitions; their interests, hobbies, and pursuits.	• Take the time to get to know them. • Inquire about their personal lives from time to time; remember names, places, and other key facts about what they are doing. • Reveal things about your personal life, too. • If possible, do some things with individuals outside of work.

TABLE 1 CONTINUED

Level	Focus of Caring	Representative Behaviors
LEVEL 7	**The families and loved ones:** you care about the other people in their lives who are important to them.	• Get to know their families and loved ones. • Socialize with them and include some of them in your life. • Attend some family events such as weddings, graduations, and birthday parties. • Be willing to help family/loved ones in ways that are appropriate.

about him or her. With some employees, no matter how much you extend yourself or try to show that you care about them and their well-being, they just don't reciprocate. In the face of their indifference, it's difficult to continue showing a high level of genuine caring for them.

So what's the right answer? First, know yourself well enough to know whom you really do care about and at what level you care. Know what you really care about and then consistently behave that way. Second, beware about caring for most employees only to a Level 2 or 3 but showing caring toward others at a Level 6 or 7. The latter will be your favorites, the former will feel like outsiders, and you may inadvertently create a caste system in your group.

I think that in most circumstances, you should strive to care for everyone who works for you at least to a Level 5. If you just don't care at that level, then don't try to fake it, but most people would consider Level 5 behaviors to be a minimum for being sensitive to others. Caring about people's health and welfare and caring about their happiness and emotional state are pretty basic measures of sensitivity. However, the level of sensitivity expected in a workplace varies by the nature of the workplace. It's fair to assume, for instance, that oil field workers have different expectations about sensitivity from their managers than workers in a hospital might have. Women may have different expectations about sensitivity than men do. For instance, women have a significantly greater need for courtesy and consideration than men do. They have a much greater need for respect from managers and a far greater need than men to feel that they are cared for. Still, we're all human, and we respond better when the people we work for are astute enough to be sensitive to what's happening in our lives and caring enough to help us when help is needed.

Get to Know People as Individuals

The best way to create caring for people is to get to know them as individuals. D. Michael Abrashoff, author of *It's Your Ship,* commanded an award-winning guided missile destroyer in the U.S. Navy.[3] In his book and speeches, he talks about his transformation as a leader. As you might imagine, the U.S. Navy is a command-and-control environment, especially aboard ships of war, but Abrashoff learned early in his tenure as the ship's captain that getting to know his crew changed both his attitude and theirs:

> I used to view them as just people to be ordered about to get a mission accomplished, to reach our bottom line. When I interviewed them and got to know them, I realized they had as much on the ball, if not more, than me. And that they wanted to do great things. They had loved ones they wanted to take care of. They had goals they wanted to achieve. I started thinking, who am I not to create the climate that helps these people achieve their goals? Before, I never knew them, never cared about them, just assumed they were out to screw me over, and I thought I had to micromanage them. But after I got to know them, I came to respect them and then wanted to help them achieve their goals.[4]

Abrashoff's record as a ship's captain is remarkable, and the lesson he learned is both simple and powerful: The more you get to know people, the more you will care about them and their lives and goals, and when they know you care about them, they will start caring about you and will work wonders to help you achieve your goals. Moreover, to become more sensitive to people, you have to be aware of their individual dreams, hopes, aspirations, attitudes, moods, feelings, and cares. So the more you get to know them, the more sensitive you are likely to become. Abrashoff's simple technique was to interview each of his crew members privately and learn about them as human beings.

Be Aware of Your Impact on People

A manager's behavior has a magnified effect on others because of the power differential between managers and those they manage. I learned this lesson when my company opened a new office and had to redecorate the space. I delegated the responsibility for getting the new office ready. It was not the sort of thing I wanted to be involved in, and I knew that Sharon, my assistant, would handle it well. One day, as I was walking through a hallway toward my office, Sharon showed me some carpet samples and asked which one I liked. Without giving it much thought, I quickly scanned the selections and picked one. Later, when the office was occupied, I learned that no one liked the carpet, and I asked Sharon why we had chosen that one. She looked at me as though I'd just landed from outer space and said, "Because that's the one you wanted!"

When you are in charge, your opinion carries more weight than you imagine. What you do and say can have great impact on the people you manage. Sometimes you want that effect. Sometimes you need to get an important message across and want people to stand up and take notice.

But now and then your words, which you may have spoken in haste and without much thought, have unintended consequences.

So consider what happens when you do the following:

1. An employee has been waiting to talk to you. You walk by the person without speaking or making eye contact.

2. In a meeting, an employee begins to give a presentation you've asked for. It isn't what you expected, and you cut the presentation short and ask that person to go back and get it right.

3. In your haste to get an apparently stalled project moving, you go around your managers and work directly with their direct reports, giving them directions and deadlines.

4. You are irritable about a family matter. At work, you are unusually gruff and abrupt with someone who comes to you with a problem.

Here is what actually happened in each of these real cases:

1. The employee's self-confidence was undermined. She thought she'd done something wrong and felt diminished by the manager's slight. Compounding the problem, that manager later berated her for not getting back to him sooner.

2. The employee was infuriated and felt embarrassed publicly. Other people who witnessed the incident agreed that this manager never gave good directions and then, when people did not deliver what he expected, criticized them for "not getting it."

3. The manager's direct reports felt micromanaged and complained that they could not do their jobs because they had no real control over the people who worked for them. They couldn't even be sure they knew what their people were working on and what priorities they'd been given.

4. People learned to fear giving this manager bad news because she tended to shoot the messenger. After a while, people stopped deliv-

ering bad news, and the manager operated in a vacuum caused by the conspiracy of silence that resulted from people not wanting to be caught in her crosshairs. She lost touch with the reality of her business and was later fired because the performance in her division was plummeting.

It's often difficult to know how your behavior is affecting the people who work for you. It's hard to be objective about yourself and impossible to see yourself as others see you. The best solution I've found is to develop confidants on your staff who are secure enough and candid enough to tell it to you like it is. You need to listen to them with an open mind, although the news they deliver may not always be what you want to hear, and then thank them for their candor.

Fix Any Problem Right Away

If you discover that something you've said or done has had unintended negative consequences, fix the problem right away. And if whatever you did caused someone grief or embarrassment in public, fix the problem publicly. Being sensitive to people means you care about how you make them feel. If you cause them grief, pain, or anxiety, you should let them know that you feel bad about it.

Know What Behaviors Offend Others and Avoid Them

You need to be cognizant of what others might find offensive, which could include sexually provocative or suggestive remarks, prejudicial comments, off-color jokes, gossip, political or religious polemics, bullying, and loud or boisterous behavior. I coached one loud, joke-telling, slap-on-the-back manager who said that he knew his behavior gave some people heartburn. "But I have to be true to myself," he told me. As I told him, it's important to be genuine, but you also need to be sensitive to other people and adaptable enough in your behavior to accommodate a wide range of people. In today's workplace, one size does not fit all. You may not be able to be your unbridled self if that means offending the people who work for you. Diversity is not just a good idea; it's today's reality. Unconscious people aren't aware of what offends others and thus they act stupidly. Narcissists, bullies, and louts often do know what offends but do it anyway. A good people person, on the other hand, is sensitive to what offends others and avoids it because offending others serves no real purpose. It just alienates them, gives them a negative impression of you, and can create resistors or opponents where you had none before. It also breeds disrespect and distrust. So what's the point of doing it?

Hold Yourself to a Higher Standard of Behavior

You should be extra vigilant about your behavior toward employees of the opposite sex. The very real sexual abuses that have taken place at work in the past (and unfortunately still occur in today's workplace) make it imperative that managers hold themselves to a higher standard of behavior and are especially careful to treat everyone with dignity and respect. It's your responsibility to create a positive and healthy work environment—and this means taking action if you see anyone being abusive or disrespectful toward other employees. Even if you are not abusive yourself, if you tolerate abuse or anything else that creates a hostile work environment, you are morally culpable and may be legally liable as well.

Listen with Your Eyes as Well as Your Ears

Many managers are well-intentioned, but they are busy and more task focused than people focused. They often have technical backgrounds and are more interested in the *what* and *how* than the *who*. As I've observed these managers interacting with others, what has been most striking to me is the extent to which they miss the visual cues other people give them. They hear the words but don't "hear" the nonverbal cues—the posture, gestures, tone, and subtle facial expressions that convey much of the speaker's meaning. As functioning adults they undoubtedly know and understand these forms of nonverbal communication, so they are probably just ignoring them for the sake of expediency.

You need to listen with your eyes as well as your ears. Much of the meaning in any spoken communication actually comes not from what the speaker says but from how he or she says it. You note the speaker's slight canting of the head, or the stress in the voice, or the unusual intonation of a word, or an unexpected pause, and these cues tell you what the speaker really means. Don't be one of those managers who either choose to ignore many of these cues or are insensitive to them. Listening with your eyes—observing those nonverbal cues and responding to them—is a key to being more sensitive in your interactions with others.

Be Sensitive about How and When You Give People Feedback

We've all heard the old bromide that feedback is a gift, but for most people it's perceived as a threat. Feedback is anxiety provoking for most people because it threatens to undermine their self-esteem. It can also have serious consequences if, as part of a poor performance appraisal, it results in a lost promotion, raise, bonus, or other potential reward. When receiving feedback, many people become defensive, even though they may outwardly seem calm and accepting of it and even grateful for it. Given how anxiety provoking feedback is, here are some suggestions for giving it sensitively.

▪ Wait before giving feedback—but don't wait too long. Don't give feedback until you have carefully thought through how to do it and how to frame your message. If you give feedback when you are angry, frustrated, or upset by something, you are likely to use stronger language than you might have intended and provoke a fight-or-flight response in the person you're giving the feedback to. But do it soon enough that people remember the event the feedback is based on and can remember what they and others did or did not do.

▪ Always give feedback from a helping heart and mind. Don't give feedback to punish someone, vent your anger or frustration, make a public display of the person's incompetence, or send a message to the rest of the group by scapegoating one person. Think of feedback as a fundamental part of coaching, with the purpose of informing, helping, educating, and building the person's skills, confidence, and esteem.

▪ Use the sandwich technique: give positive feedback first, then the corrective feedback, and then end with more positives. Most people find negative feedback easier to receive if it also comes with positive feedback—some sugar with the bitter pill, so to speak. Likewise, many managers find it easier to give negative feedback if they can begin and end with positives. This is especially true of nurturing managers, who may be reluctant to give negative feedback at all because it seems to violate their nurturing side.

▪ Frame your message carefully. Choose your words wisely. Most people are very sensitive to the words others use and the tone in which those words are spoken. You can strain an otherwise good relationship if you choose your words poorly. On one occasion, I overheard a manager giving feedback to an employee and saying, "What you did was really dumb." Using a word such as "dumb" to characterize an employee's actions adds an emotional layer to the conversation that doesn't need to be there. It can offend people and make them so defensive they don't hear or accept the message.

■ Don't surprise people with negative feedback. Let them know in advance that you want to talk about the event and give them time to reflect on it themselves. Of course, it's best when people recognize that they didn't do their best and ask for feedback or coaching. But if they don't, then find a quiet, private place to discuss their performance and allow them to be prepared mentally before you give the feedback.

The research on what people want shows that receiving feedback from managers is crucial to virtually all types of employees. Seventy-eight percent of men and 83 percent of women indicated that constructive feedback from managers is highly important to them. But employees want more than feedback. Many also want encouragement, advice, and coaching. In the research, 56 percent of men said they wanted advice from their managers (for women, the figure was 51 percent). More than 70 percent of men had a high need for encouragement from their managers and an equal number wanted their managers to act as coaches or mentors. The figures for women were nearly identical. The majority of employees want managers who are devoted to helping them develop their skills and capabilities.

Don't Be Brutally Honest If That Means Hurting People

There is nothing wrong with being candid and forthright. You should be. But there are better and worse ways to say, "I have a problem with you" or "I don't like the way you did that." You gain nothing worthwhile by hurting people with candor if you can be candid with them in a way that validates their basic humanity and shows kindness on your part.

Don't be proud about saying whatever is on your mind if that is hurtful to others. There's no excuse for that kind of insensitivity, especially if you are the manager.

Let People Save Face

To the extent possible, let people feel good about themselves. Let them triumph. Give them opportunities to shine, and avoid doing things that diminish their self-esteem. People want to feel good about themselves. If you can help them do that in ways that are genuine, they will repay you with loyalty and commitment. This is especially true if they know that you have made a choice and been generous in your treatment of them and positive in your regard for them.

Tips for Improving Your Relationships

1. Behave gracefully toward other people.

2. Be sensitive (but not hypersensitive) to deviations from the norm.

3. Distinguish between a person's being and his or her current behavior.

4. Show empathy when others reveal their feelings.

5. Don't fake caring.

6. Care for the people who work for you.

7. Get to know people as individuals.

8. Be aware of your impact on people.

9. Fix any problem right away.

10. Know what behaviors offend others and avoid them.

11. Hold yourself to a higher standard of behavior.

12. Listen with your eyes as well as your ears.

13. Be sensitive about how and when you give people feedback.

14. Don't be brutally honest if that means hurting people.

15. Let people save face.

5 Respecting Others

Everyone deserves respect, because they are human, because whatever their differences from us they are part of the human journey, part of our common origin and development as a species. But they don't deserve *unconditional* respect. Some respect— such as respect for their ideas, contributions, and achievements—has to be earned. For example, I may respect someone's humanity but still not respect his choices, behaviors, values, affiliations, and performance (or lack of them). In short, I am obliged to respect someone because he is a person, but I am not obliged to respect him no matter what he does or fails to do. He has to earn some of my respect. I will discuss these two kinds of respect, what I call *inherent respect* and *earned respect*, and I will suggest ways in which you can show both types.

Inherent Respect

We respect other people because they share our journey. No matter who they are, they have a journey that in many respects is like mine. They struggle in many of the ways I struggle. They have hopes, fears, loves, dreams, and doubts, as I do. Their perspective may be different from mine, but I respect their right to have a perspective. And if I am a decent human being, I will treat them with dignity simply because they are human.

If I show inherent respect toward others, I respect their individuality as well as our commonality. In other words, I respect the ways we are similar but also the many ways in which we are different. I respect his right to be different and her right to have her own identity. Likewise, I respect each person's right to privacy. But respecting others who are different from ourselves is not always easy, especially when they are from a different culture.

Respect for Other Cultures

We tend to prejudge people and respect or disrespect them for often spurious reasons—ones that have far more to do with us than with them. Twenty years ago some colleagues and I designed an interpersonal skills workshop for management consultants. To help the participants appreciate individual differences and the biases they take into relationships with people of various cultures, we created an exercise in which each person received a laminated card that described the typical behaviors, attitudes, or beliefs of his or her culture. We then had the participants pair with someone from a culture other than their own and conduct an initial meeting between a client and a consultant. To avoid assumptions based on real human cultures, we wrote role cards based on fictitious planetary cultures: Mercury, Venus, Mars, Neptune, Jupiter, Saturn, Xenon, Krypton, and Boc-Roc. Here, for example, were the instructions for people belonging to the Xenon and Neptune cultures:

Xenon

You are from the culture Xenon. In your culture, people greet one another enthusiastically. To do otherwise is considered an insult. You typically grasp the other person's hands with both of yours and shake vigorously.

In your culture, it is impolite to discuss business without first asking about the other person's family. When you do start talking about business, it is usually to structure the discussion around the overall goal and aspirations for the work in an inspiring way. Xenonites frequently synthesize the discussion by drawing analogies to the family (e.g., "We will work together closely like twins").

Xenonites are very demonstrative, so you should use broad hand and arm gestures, exaggerate your facial expressions, and be animated when you talk. To do otherwise would imply that you are not interested in the other person.

Neptune

You are from the culture Neptune. As a Neptunian, you consider it impolite to look others in the eye when you speak to them. However, you must look them in the eye when they speak to you. So whenever you speak, you must look away (typically, you cast your eyes downward and look at the floor).

Neptunians generally structure a business conversation by first disclosing the facts they know, expecting the other person to do the same thing. They seek a shared synthesis of the conversation by politely asking if there are any further important facts that need to be addressed.

Neptunians consider the left hand to be offensive (it is thought to be the hand of aggression), so you must keep your left hand out of sight at all times. If the other person reveals his or her left hand, you instinctively move away slightly. And if the other person should wave his or her left hand, you would take offense and rise and back away quickly.

As you can see, when a Xenonite meets a Neptunian, there is a strong potential for misunderstanding and conflict, regardless of the content of their conversation. It should be obvious that the cultural behaviors we chose for these two planets are based on a mixture of actual cultural expectations and behaviors in societies around the world. When we ran this workshop exercise, the participants discovered that they often misinterpreted, misjudged, and mistrusted their counterparts. They were suspicious of the others and could not understand why they were behaving the way they were. In many cases, the role plays were hilarious as one person sought to be closer and the other instinctively moved away. The participants learned a number of powerful lessons about trust and respect through this exercise.

- First, you won't respect someone if you don't trust the person—at least not completely. Respect is based in part on mutual trust and understanding.

- We give more trust and respect to people who are like us. To the degree that they are unlike us, we tend to distrust and disrespect them. People who are like us validate our own assumptions about what is right or wrong, proper or improper, acceptable or unacceptable.

- We tend to be suspicious toward behaviors, attitudes, and beliefs we don't understand, however natural they might be to the people from those cultures. When we don't understand something, we tend to attribute negative motives to it. For instance, the people from cultures that maintain steady eye contact often assumed that someone from another culture that avoids steady eye contact was devious and dishonest. "He seemed to be hiding something," they would often say in the debriefing after the exercise.

- We have trouble liking someone who is not like us, especially if their behaviors seem crazy or stupid to us. Culturally different behavior, by itself, is enough to cause feelings of suspicion, distrust, and the early stages of hatred.

▪ It is difficult sometimes to get beneath the level of behaviors and apparent attitudes. We form impressions based on initial, surface impressions, and from that point on we tend to hear and see only what confirms those initial impressions. In short, once you start disliking and distrusting someone who is different from you, it's difficult to turn that around.

▪ Respect for people is based in part on how similar they are to us. We hold them in higher regard if they reinforce and reflect our own cultural assumptions and behaviors, and vice versa.

One of the key lessons from this exercise is that the most potent barriers to developing stronger relationships with people who are different from us in some way are our own biases, assumptions, and predispositions. We view others from behind our own cultural lens, and we tend to judge them negatively if they differ from us in inexplicable ways.

Here are some ways you can show inherent respect for people.

Respect Individual and Cultural Differences

To respect others you have to respect individual and cultural differences. What makes this challenging for many people is that embracing difference may imply that we and our group or clan are not as special as we thought we were. We humans want to think that we're right, that our beliefs are correct, that our team is superior, that our group is better, that we are the chosen ones, that our god is the one true god, that we work for the best company or live in the best place, that our values are the correct ones. We devote considerable time and energy to being distinctively better in some way than *others*—those who are *not us*. We want to win, and for *us* to win, *they* have to lose. The *they* in this case is anyone who threatens our self-concept or self-esteem. If I accept that people who are different from me—having different backgrounds, making different assumptions, holding different beliefs—could be right, then wouldn't that make me wrong?

To respect differences, including cultural differences, means to accept people as they are, perhaps even to celebrate who they are; to celebrate your own differences as well as theirs; to seek to understand, appreciate, and even leverage diversity. I've seen managers do it by celebrating Cinco de Mayo with their Latino employees, by inviting people to share something proud about their ethnic background during brown bag lunches, by asking the amateur photographers in the company to do photographic essays on their families or neighborhoods or others who share their ethnic origins. There are countless creative ways to celebrate diversity and create an inclusive environment. At the same time, as a manager you cannot tolerate behavior among any employees—or customers—that is discriminatory or prejudicial. The moment you see it or hear about it, you have to deal swiftly and perhaps publicly with the offense. Then you send a message that embracing diversity and being inclusive are absolutes in your organization.

It goes without saying that you have to behave inclusively and generously with everyone who works for you or seeks to work for you. Your hiring processes, performance appraisals, compensation practices and policies, and other human resource actions must reflect respect for individual and cultural differences. You have to model what you expect from others, and your behavior must reflect a higher standard.

Put Yourself in the Other Person's Shoes

I once worked with a manager who described himself as a "reformed bigot." I was surprised to hear him call himself that and asked him to explain. He said that he had been raised in a traditional family with strong opinions about everyone, especially members of other ethnic groups, who were typically described as being lazy, stupid, criminal, and entitlement minded. When he got into the workforce, he had to work with many people from these ethnic groups and found that unless he changed his mind about them he would fail, as an employee and particularly as a manager. To force his own mind-set shift, he put some of these people in key positions or had them sit on key committees or task forces. Then he asked for their perspectives on the pertinent business issues and forced himself to listen without judgment or interruption.

Initially, he found himself making assumptions about what they would say and whether they would be right or wrong in their judgments. As he became more savvy, he learned to just listen, to appreciate the employees' perspectives for what they were, and to ask probing questions to understand what lay beneath those perspectives. From understanding came acceptance and enlightenment, and the performance of his business unit improved, because he was able to apply the insights he learned in product development, marketing, sales, and customer service. To really get to know someone, he said, you have to ask them, "What's it like for you? How do you experience this?" Sometimes, what he heard was hard to take (e.g., "This is just another way you people marginalize us. You say you care but you don't"), and he found it hard to listen without becoming defensive or aggressive in return. But when people saw that he was genuinely interested in knowing how they felt, they opened up more and began to work with him on constructive changes in the workplace. They became engaged in the solution because they saw that he was engaged in the problem and genuinely wanted to hear what they thought.

Whenever you find yourself not understanding someone or not appreciating the person's choices, try to put yourself in her shoes. How would the situation look to you then? If you're not sure, ask the person how it looks to her and then listen carefully. After you get to know someone, here are some questions you might ask in casual conversation to probe more deeply.

- ▪ What do you hope for?
- ▪ What do you wish would go away?
- ▪ What is important to you?
- ▪ What do you value?
- ▪ What are your dreams?
- ▪ What do you love doing?
- ▪ What do you hate doing?
- ▪ What do you find most/least satisfying about your job/work?

When you can ask these kinds of questions you will discover a richer, deeper, more interesting person than you might have guessed.

Take No for an Answer

You show respect for someone when you take no for an answer. I was tickling a granddaughter once, and she asked me to stop. I did so immediately because I wanted her to know that she could set boundaries and have those boundaries respected. Likewise, when she gets too rambunctious with me and I ask her to stop, I expect her to do so right away, so she knows that other people also have boundaries that must be respected.

An important part of respecting others is being willing to take no for an answer. Of course, we have to distinguish between situations where employees should not say no (when they are given a legitimate assignment, for instance) and situations where their personal boundaries are being crossed (e.g., when they are asked to do something illegal or unethical or when the request is personal, as when a boss repeatedly asks an employee for a date and the employee is not interested). A number of cases involving allegations of sexual harassment involve situations where a manager has not been willing to take no for an answer. Don't assume that someone is being coy if you ask them for something personal and they ask you to stop—or even behave as though they are not interested in your inquiries or advances. Respecting people means hearing no when people say no and respecting that.

Avoid Making Examples of People

You respect people when you preserve their dignity and avoid turning them into examples of what not to do. We've probably all known bosses who felt that reprimanding people in public was useful because it let everyone else know in a public way how not to behave. I've heard the following kinds of comments in recent years.

- "Joe, you sure screwed that up."
- "We fell well short of our target this month because the western region reps could not get their act together."
- "Let's be candid here. Kay's group failed to do its job, and everybody knows it."
- "I don't mean to single you out, Larry, but you had the worst return rate of anyone on the team last month. If you don't get off your butt, you're not going to be around here much longer."

Never use public occasions, like all-company or group meetings, to give negative feedback to someone, criticize them, denigrate another group or business unit, or otherwise throw the spotlight on someone you want to single out for punishment. Once you do that, people will question your judgment as well as your motives and will learn to be wary of you. Instilling fear in some people may work, but it's not good leadership. So if you are going to correct someone or give them negative feedback, do it in private.

Earned Respect

We tend to respect people not for what they've been given but for what they've done with it, not for their gifts but for their accomplishments.

Some highly gifted people don't deserve respect because they squander their gifts, take them for granted, or behave arrogantly because they possess what others don't. We admire people who have had to struggle, to overcome great odds, not those who were exceptionally lucky or were "in the right place at the right time." We respect hard work, perseverance, resilience, defiance in the face of resistance, and courage confronting insurmountable odds. We don't admire the beautifully born as much as the plain Johns and Janes who have made more of themselves than they were given. We might envy (or resent) those who have inherited beauty or wealth, but we don't respect them simply because of their inheritances.

We also respect people's contributions, the value they create in the workplace or outside of it. We respect the successful application of knowledge and skills. We respect hard work and what it can produce, and we respect personal growth and development. We admire people who have struggled at night and on weekends to earn another college degree while raising a family, become certified in some professional or technical specialty, or otherwise attain something of merit that required time, dedication, and personal sacrifice to achieve. Lastly, we admire hardworking, dedicated employees who apply themselves daily, remain focused, are diligent, and have a personal commitment to doing the finest work they can. We admire people who get excellent results consistently.

In some respects, the most important job you have is to recognize the contributions of your good-to-great performers. It motivates them, encourages others, establishes your standards, and communicates that you care and you share. Giving credit where credit is due is simple, profoundly effective, and very motivating to your entire team. It adds as much energy to your team as your hogging all the credit would take away.

Here are some ways you can show earned respect.

Give Rewards, Recognition, and Celebrations

Here are some ways you can show respect by giving people rewards and recognition:

- Recognize them publicly for their work.

- Feature their work prominently in summaries of your group's contributions.

- Reward people appropriately for their contributions by giving them merit increases, bonuses, time off, and so on.

- Celebrate their accomplishments in group or company meetings or informal get-togethers, by naming something after them (at Lore, we recognized a superior consultant by naming a meeting room after him) or by giving them special one-of-a-kind awards.

- Give them the credit in front of senior management (be sure they are present so senior managers can congratulate them in person).

- Share their work with others, especially people outside your group (e.g., by having them give part of the presentation to other groups instead of you giving the whole presentation).

Delegate and Get People Involved

Here are some ways you can show respect by delegating to people and getting them involved:

- Assign them work that builds on their contributions and recognizes their expertise (you have to ensure that they know they are receiving a special assignment because of their extraordinary contributions in the past).

- Ask for their help or advice on matters related to their expertise.

▪ Ask them to participate on committees, task forces, or work teams where their work adds value.

▪ Help them network with the right people inside and outside your company.

▪ Defer to their judgment when you are discussing their area of expertise.

▪ Ask for and listen to their opinions (the surest sign is to implement something they've suggested).

▪ Involve them in problem solving and key decisions; delegate some responsibilities to them.

▪ Promote them into positions that recognize their contributions and leverage the value they bring to the company.

Encourage People to Share Their Ideas

People also earn respect through the quality and quantity of their ideas and dreams. I worked once with a line manager in an aerospace company whom I'll call Gene. Gene was an excellent manager in virtually all respects, but he lacked imagination. A nose-to-the-grindstone type of guy, Gene kept people focused on the tasks at hand. The people in his group who aspired to something more than what they were currently doing found that he wasn't interested. If it didn't pertain to getting the current job done, Gene just didn't want to hear it. He also had no patience for people's personal dreams, including those of the employee whose son was a talented pianist and wanted a flexible schedule so she could travel with her son to some performances. Gene told her she would have to figure it out on her own, and if she couldn't do that he could find someone else to do her job.

Contrast Gene with Everett, a manager in another aerospace firm. Everett believed that if people merely worked to pay their bills they would be only about half as productive as they were capable of being. But if they worked to satisfy some of their deepest longings, they would amaze you with their productivity. So he sought employees who wanted to work there, who wanted to do what they were doing, and he emphasized how their work contributed to the whole of what his unit and the company produced. He fostered pride and advocated that people dream large and follow their dreams. Mind you, Everett also ran a tight ship. He was every bit the manager Gene was, but Everett found the sweet spot in people's hopes, and they would have followed him into hell had he asked them to do it. Everett knew what each of his employees aspired to become, what got them excited—from the man who wanted to be a world-class bridge player (Everett encouraged him to set up a lunch-hour bridge group) to the woman who wanted to get into local politics (Everett sponsored her in Toastmasters and contributed to her city council campaign).

As you know, some employees do their jobs well but without inspiration. They know the drill and do it with relative ease. If they have ideas, they don't bother to share them. Businesses probably need some of these plodders. They get the job done and mostly get it right. But you won't build a winning enterprise if that's all you have. You also need the curious, the creative, the restless—the ones who don't agree with how things have always been done and are willing to be vocal about it. They keep life interesting. Even if their ideas are not always great, you want to encourage them to keep thinking, dreaming, and scheming. You want them to be unhappy—in the right way. You want them unhappy with the status quo, unhappy with processes that are too cumbersome, unhappy with results that don't increase the customer's satisfaction. Encourage these people by showing that you respect, first, their right (even obligation) to speak up, and then the quality of their ideas when those ideas have merit.

You have to beware of falling into the automatic response: "Oh, what a great idea! I'll think about it and get back to you." Of course, the managers who say this are using the response as a placeholder to avoid seriously discussing lousy ideas, and pretty soon everyone knows that "What a great idea!" is a sure sign that the manager hated it but was reluctant to be candid for fear of offending someone. When someone offers a lousy or marginal idea, here are some possible ways to respond that are honest and not deflating.

■ That's an interesting idea. I especially like the built-in feedback loop with our customers, but we've tried it before. Several years ago, we implemented something very similar, and it fell apart after about six months. Walt could tell you more about it. Although it seemed promising at the time, it didn't work because of . . . Why don't you give it more thought, talk to Walt about it, and see if you can think of a way around the drawbacks that stopped us when we tried something like this before.

■ I like how your idea would appear to solve the late delivery problem, but I'm concerned that quality will suffer if we eliminate these two steps. How would you ensure that quality would either remain the same, which is darned good, or even improve?

These responses acknowledge the idea, express what's good or positive about it, indicate why it may not work or hasn't worked previously, and invite the person to do more thinking about his or her proposed solution. But when people do offer ideas of genuine merit, you need to acknowledge that merit and then invite them to participate in developing the ideas further.

If You Have Erred, Be Willing to Apologize

No one is perfect, including you. If you err in a relationship, be the first to offer an apology. I've known many managers who were too proud or too stubborn to admit that they were wrong, had spoken too harshly, had been mixed up, or had otherwise done something that caused someone else discomfort or embarrassment. You are holding yourself to the higher standard when you take the lead in apologizing and trying to make things right. Pride is foolish if it causes harm to someone else and can be rectified so easily by your gracious acknowledgement that you erred.

You should be the first to apologize if you have erred, but what if you haven't? In that case, it can be dangerous to apologize. First, it's not authentic and on some level the other person will know that and will thereafter suspect that you will say anything in order to smooth things over. Second, some people try to avoid responsibility by shifting the blame to others. If you apologize for something you didn't do, you play into their blame-shifting behavior and allow them to get away with it. If you have contributed to the problem or have miscommunicated or misunderstood what has been said, then it's fair to accept some responsibility for the problem and apologize for that. However, it's best in the long run to insist on complete honesty and acceptance of responsibility all around.

Remember That What Works for You Does Not Necessarily Work for Others

We view reality through our own lens. What we believe to be true is filtered through our experiences, operating style, wants, needs, biases, and deepest desires. Consequently, our version of truth varies from every other person's version of truth. Moreover, throughout our lives each of us has developed a unique set of skills, shortcuts, rules of thumb, and ways of working that succeed for us (or else we wouldn't do or use them repeatedly). We typically offer these personal learnings in the form of advice: "If I were you, I would . . ." or "What has always worked for me is . . ." It's not that we shouldn't offer others advice, but we have to avoid assuming that it's the only way to do things and that what has worked for us will work for them. You are more respectful toward others when you acknowledge that their way of doing things is probably better for them and that they have to discover for themselves what will work best for them (perhaps with some suggestions from you on what they might try).

Respect What You Don't Know

We often have sideways conversations with another person because the two of us have different facts, are making different assumptions, or have differing priorities—and neither of us knows it. Our tendency in these circumstances is to assume that the other person is being difficult, obtuse, or contrary for reasons we can't fathom. It's best to trust that the other person is operating with benign intent and doing the best they can. You may not know what's causing their behavior or leading them to think or say something that seems peculiar, but avoid the trap of assuming that something is wrong with them. Instead, trust that what's driving them makes sense. Seek to understand what lies beneath their actions or words and then, if necessary, discuss your differences or provide coaching or education. Similarly, if someone is resisting a direction or decision and you can't figure out why, it's often good to ask, "What would make you feel more comfortable?" Then you are enjoining them to participate in the problem solving and to get at the heart of what's troubling them about the direction you're asking them to take. When I've done this, we've nearly always resolved the issues within minutes— and without compromising what I was trying to accomplish.

When You Have Little Chemistry with Someone, Respect What You Can Learn from Them

This is a tricky suggestion because when we don't have good chemistry with someone else, our fondest wish is to avoid them or limit our dealings with them, which may or may not be possible. But there is something to be learned from every interaction and every person you work with, even those whom you don't like and don't particularly want to deal with. I do think it's true that we have something to learn from everyone—*if* we are open to the learning. You can say to yourself, "I don't know what I'm supposed to learn from this person, but I'm sure he or she is in my life for some reason. What is it?"

Tips for Improving Your Relationships

1. Respect individual and cultural differences.

2. Put yourself in the other person's shoes.

3. Take no for an answer.

4. Avoid making examples of people.

5. Give rewards, recognition, and celebrations.

6. Delegate and get people involved.

7. Encourage people to share their ideas.

8. If you have erred, be willing to apologize. (If you haven't erred, beware of apologizing.)

9. Remember that what works for you does not necessarily work for others.

10. Respect what you don't know.

11. When you have little chemistry with someone, respect what you can learn from them.

6 | Making It Personal

Karen McKibbin reminisces about her grandmother, Dorothy McKibbin, who ran the Santa Fe office of the Manhattan Project during World War II for J. Robert Oppenheimer. When she was a child, Karen spent hours sitting with her grandmother on a park bench in Santa Fe and watching people. They would see a woman and wonder what her journey had been, where she was raised, whether her parents were still alive and what they were doing, what she had done with her life, what mattered to her, what she dreamed about, and so on. They would notice the crow's-feet around a man's eyes and wonder, what did it mean? Had he been out in the sun too much? Was it his genes? Or worry? If so, what was he worried about? Good people persons like Dorothy McKibbin are curious about what's happening in other people's lives. They also tend to be generous. Dorothy McKibbin welcomed many people into her home—friends and strangers alike. She called it "opening my life to other people."[1]

Like Dorothy McKibbin, good managers are curious about the people who work for them. Beyond knowing what skills and experience people have, they want to know what drives them, what they want to accomplish, what they like and don't like doing, what they are interested in after work, what they do to have fun, what they do to celebrate, how close they are to family, what they aspire to become. The managers who are best at developing employee relationships remember the important facts about people's lives and inquire about them from time to time. They call people by their first name, send cards on their birthday, and celebrate important occasions. In short, they make it personal.

Here are some ways you can make it personal.

Treat Employees Like Human Beings, Not Human Resources

Making it personal means that you treat people like people and not like resources, objects, or tools to be used to achieve your goals. I've met some managers who didn't remember people's names (because it didn't matter to them), who kept people at arm's length because they didn't want to endure the "messiness" of dealing with people, who treated people like objects on a balance sheet. One manager I worked with, Charles, literally thought of people as entries on a balance sheet. "This guy has some serious liabilities," he would say about someone working for him, "but he gets the job done. But this other guy is a huge asset. I need to leverage him more."

I met another man, a partner in a large management consulting firm, who thought of the associates in his office as being green lights, yellow lights, or red lights. The green lights were definite winners, the red lights losers, and the yellow lights maybes. He told me that he mentored and encouraged the green lights, ignored the red lights, and spent coaching time with the yellow lights when he had spare moments, which was rare. I have no doubt that the dehumanizing way he treated subordinates discouraged many of them and led to suboptimal performance. Why would people continue to try hard if they felt prejudged and looked down upon? Treating people like traffic lights is not conducive to building strong, productive, energizing relationships with your employees.

Invariably, if you treat people like human resources, they will know it and will not feel loyal to you. If they continue to work for you, it won't be because they care about you. You will likely be nothing more than a meal ticket to them, and they will not give you the energy, time, creativity, and commitment that could make a difference—often a *substantial* difference—in how your unit performs and how your customers are treated. It's wise to remember that, at least at work, loyalty is nearly always personal, especially today when people have more choices about where they can work. People are loyal to causes and driven by a passionate commitment to ideals, but in the workplace they are rarely loyal to a leader or even a company unless they believe in that leader or company and because their personal and professional needs are being met. Which needs? The ones I'm writing about in this book. People are loyal to those leaders who treat them the way they want to be treated. If you aren't curious about them, if you don't care, if you don't make it personal, they will be far less likely to care about you. Why should they?

Remember People's Names

The most fundamental and dearest thing people own is their identity. You humanize both the other person and yourself when you call someone by name. Making an effort to remember someone's name is a sign that you care, that he or she isn't merely a job function to you (e.g., the broker on the third floor in the corner office or the tall guy in shipping). If you're like me and don't remember names easily, you have to make a special effort to do that.

Beyond just remembering people's names, you need to know what they prefer to be called. Is it Michael or Mike or Mikey? John, Johnny, or Jack? Debra, Deborah, Debby, or Deb? Christina, Christy, Crissy, Chris, or Tina? And is it spelled Carla or Karla, Jean or Jeanne, Debby or Debbie, Clark or Clarke? These distinctions matter. Not taking the time to get it right is a sign of indifference. If you aren't sure, ask. Asking shows that you care about getting it right and respect the person's identity and individuality.

Remember People's Birthdays and Celebrate Them

I make a point of sending birthday cards to everyone in my company—on their birthday, of course! In a company of Lore's size, I can't remember everyone's birthday, so my assistant keeps track of those dates and gives me a set of cards to sign at the beginning of every month. I take the time to write a personal message in each card and, if I can, hand-deliver people's cards. I do this because a person's birthday is a special day. It's a celebration of that person's existence. Whatever else happens for them on that day, I want the people working in my company to know that I care about their special day and wish them well. In the years since I've been doing this, I've been surprised at the number of times I've seen those cards on people's desks or thumbtacked to a bulletin board in their office long after their birthday passed. Birthday cards are small gestures with huge impact.

You could also send flowers or balloons, take the birthday celebrants to lunch, have cake and ice cream brought in, hold an office party for them, or give them that day off. Or you could do something more creative. I once worked with a man named Larry who wore unusual, loud, and sometimes bizarre ties to work. It became his hallmark. So for his birthday one year, we held a surprise wear-a-Larry-like-tie-to-work contest. On his birthday, we invited Larry's coworkers to wear the most outrageous necktie they could make, find, or buy. Larry was the judge, and the winner received—you guessed it—a truly awful necktie. I'm not sure that Larry ever had a more memorable birthday than that one, and it created a tremendous amount of fun and team spirit. Events like these make it personal.

Ask about People's Lives and Remember the Facts

Beyond remembering people's names and birthdays, you make it personal by remembering the facts about their lives: spouse's and children's names, anniversaries or other special dates, the sports team they follow, types of pets and their names, where they went to school, their hobbies, memorable vacations, favorite foods, and so on. I've known managers who were gifted at remembering the minutiae of people's lives. Most of us aren't so gifted and have to write things down in our little black books. However you do it, remembering some facts about people's lives and asking about them from time to time is a huge relationship builder—as long as you respect people's boundaries and make no judgments about their lives. You shouldn't, for instance, ask an employee about his weekend, learn that he played poker at a casino, and then comment about the evils of gambling. Or learn that he cooked Italian food for a dinner party with friends and say that you hate Italian food because it's too fattening.

Great relationship builders care about the details of other people's lives. They care about what matters to others, what their interests and hobbies are, their likes and dislikes, their experiences and their plans. To truly connect with people, you have to connect with their gripes and their dreams. You have to know what bothers them and what excites them, what turns them off and what turns them on.

Have One Deeper Level of Curiosity about What Someone Tells You

The trick I've learned is to have at least one deeper level of curiosity about what someone tells you. Here's what I mean:

Employee: We went to the art museum this weekend. It was okay, but I've seen better.

Manager: [The pat response] Sorry to hear that. Have you checked the manifest on that shipment to Brisbane?

Manager: [One deeper level of curiosity] Sorry to hear that. We haven't gone to the exhibit yet. What did you find disappointing about it?

■ ■ ■

Employee: We went hiking this weekend. We did the Colorado Trail, which was great.

Manager: [The pat response] Sounds nice. I've hiked that trail several times.

Manager: [One deeper level of curiosity] Sounds nice. I've hiked that trail several times. What do you like most about that hike?

You don't have to be insanely curious about everything people say. You don't have time. Just one deeper level of curiosity is sufficient to show interest and learn a great deal about people—and what they say may be compelling enough to pique your curiosity even more. What was disappointing about the art museum? Why was it disappointing to this person? What did he or she expect? Conversely, what made the Colorado Trail special? Why did this person enjoy it so much? The answers will tell you a lot about the person you're talking to. Interestingly, having one deeper level of curiosity about what people tell you makes you a more interesting person to them, and it gives you a lot of insight into the people who work for you. It also shows that you care enough to be curious about them.

To Form Deeper Bonds, Disclose More about Yourself

Some managers seem to have an impenetrable facade. They reveal nothing about themselves, tell no personal stories, air no complaints, share no passions. Nor do they inquire about others, at least beyond the most superficial level. They act as though they work in a sterile environment and can't risk contaminating themselves with anything not directly related to the tasks at hand. They make their employee relationships so impersonal that no one could possibly be invested in doing more than complying with the minimum job requirements and doing what has to be done to keep from being noticed.

You build good relationships if you not only inquire about others but disclose things about yourself as well. You have to approach personal disclosure carefully. In some cultures, too much personal disclosure too quickly is off-putting to people, and they may question your motives. Americans tend to be fairly quick to disclose, while in other cultures people may wait until they get to know someone better before opening up. Still, as a general rule, you won't be able to form stronger relationships with employees unless you are willing to open up to people to the extent that it is culturally acceptable. The point is to make it personal—within limits—on both sides. (I'll talk more about the limits later in the chapter.)

Take Time to Get to Know People

You can't really make it personal unless you invest time getting to know people, and this means taking time away from the daily demands of the business and its deadlines, projects, business meetings, progress reviews, and so on. Don't have an agenda or purpose other than listening and getting to know people, and let people know that. Otherwise, they'll be waiting for you to say whatever it is you came to say. Because of the power differential between you and the people you manage, and because they know you are busy, they will assume you have some reason for coming to talk to them, especially if you haven't done this kind of thing before. You'll need to reassure them that things are fine and you're just there to get to know them better. I worked with one manager who tried this but insisted on sending a list of questions to employees ahead of time—and it absolutely backfired on her. In fact, people's suspicions grew when she insisted that she had no agenda.

In my experience, it works best to take people to breakfast or lunch. Make it as casual as possible, and don't talk about business unless you must. Even then, keep the business to a minimum. If the person takes the opportunity to raise business-related issues or concerns, be insanely curious and ask lots of questions but refrain from responding in depth or lecturing. Just listen—and take notes. Another good opportunity to get to know people is on business trips, on the airplane or in the rental car or after work in a lounge. The best time to connect with people on a more personal level is when they are relaxed and know that you are, too.

A good opening question when you take time out with people is a simple "How are you doing?" It's nonthreatening, and it allows the other person to decide how to respond, how much to disclose, and how personal to become in the ensuing conversation. This question suggests that you care how the person is doing (depending on your tone of voice), but it's nonintrusive because it permits superficial as well as thoughtful responses. From that opening, you follow the person's lead. Following are some examples that assume that the manager and employee have been working together for several years and have a good relationship:

Manager:	How are you doing, Sara?
Sara:	Oh fine. No problems.
Manager:	I'm glad to hear it.
Sara:	Do you have any idea when they're going to install the operating system upgrades?
Manager:	The upgrades are being phased in. They start on our group next Tuesday.

In this dialogue, Sara declines the manager's invitation to do anything more than talk about business, so the manager talks about business and does not probe further. However, if Sara had not been herself lately, had seemed withdrawn or depressed, or had been cranky with her colleagues, the manager might have probed further:

Manager:	How are you doing, Sara?
Sara:	Oh fine. No problems.
Manager:	I'm glad to hear it, although you haven't seemed like yourself lately.
Sara:	How so?
Manager:	Well, you just seem down. Is everything all right?
Sara:	Yeah, it'll be fine. Don't worry about it. I'm okay. But thanks for asking.

If Sara's performance has been declining or if she's not working well with her teammates, the manager has a right to probe further. Here, Sara clearly has something going on in her life that's causing her a problem, but she's not willing to talk about it yet (and maybe never). At this point, unless her performance is really problematic, the manager should let it go but remain watchful and raise the issue again if Sara's temperament and performance don't improve. But the dialogue might also have gone like this:

Manager: How are you doing, Sara?

Sara: Oh fine. No problems.

Manager: I'm glad to hear it, although you haven't seemed like yourself lately.

Sara: How so?

Manager: Well, you just seem down. Is everything all right?

Sara: Yeah, it'll be fine. I just have an issue at home. (pause) Last week, we found out that my husband has skin cancer on his hand. They think they found it early enough to stop it, but I've been worried sick. We both have.

Manager: Sara, I'm really sorry. That's not the kind of news you ever want to hear about a loved one. What can we do to be helpful?

When you ask the question, "How are you doing?" you have to listen with both your ears and your eyes. Watch how the person responds. Notice his or her body language, and listen to the tone of voice as well as the words. You learn a tremendous amount about people when you observe their responses carefully, and that question offers them the chance to open up with you if they choose to. It's really remarkable where this simple question can take you, and you often learn not only what's troubling people but what's animating them as well:

Manager: How are you doing?

Sara: Fantastic. We found out last night that my daughter's having another baby.

Manager: That's great news, Sara. So that will be four grandchildren for you?

Sara:	Yep, unless she has twins. They run in my family, so there's a good chance.
Manager:	Well, we're going to have to celebrate your wonderful news.

When Appropriate, Invest in People's Lives

When people feel that their company supports them and their dreams, they become far more committed and loyal to the company and the managers who make that happen. Several years ago, Martin Moller, one of Lore's consultants, had the opportunity to produce an off-off-Broadway play being directed by his wife, a theater professor at Fort Lewis College. It was a rare honor for the theater department in this small college to have a play performed at La MaMa Experimental Theatre Club in New York, and they needed to raise a lot of money and handle thousands of details to realize this dream. During the eight months from acceptance to production, the company supported Martin with donations of money, frequent flyer miles, volunteers, and time off to accomplish what, for Martin and his family, was a once-in-a-lifetime opportunity. We supported him, not for selfish reasons, but because he is a valued member of our team and because helping him realize this dream was the right thing to do.

I don't know that you can support every personal dream of every employee, but I think you have to do your best. When your company supports employees who run marathons for charity or gather toys for disadvantaged children during holidays or contribute to shelters for the homeless, you create a community instead of a workplace. People begin to think of their colleagues as part of their extended families, and their loyalty and commitment grow. Helping people achieve their dreams, fulfill their needs, or give back to society makes it personal in ways people find richly rewarding.

Be Generous to the People Who Work for You

Some years ago, one of Lore's professionals and his wife wanted to start a family but for medical reasons could not conceive a child, so they decided to adopt. Greg and MaryJane found an orphanage in Russia that had two boys about four years old who needed a family. But the $25,000 they needed was more than they could afford, so he decided to borrow the money wherever he could. We knew of the couple's dreams of starting a family, and when Greg asked if the company would loan him some part of that total, we said, without hesitation, that we would give him the entire amount as a no-interest loan to be paid over whatever period of time worked for him. While Greg and MaryJane were in Russia to adopt the boys, his colleagues filled the living room in his house with toys and boys' clothing as welcoming gifts for their new children. Today, they have two fine sons who have become thoroughly acclimated to America.

You don't do these sorts of things as a strategy for building employee loyalty. You do them because being generous with your people is the right thing to do. Loyalty is a natural by-product of that generosity, however. The bonds you form by helping valued employees start a family or otherwise enrich their personal lives are very strong. Generosity is one of those intangibles that make employees feel that you are worth working for.

Be Generous to the Less Fortunate

You also make your company worth working for when you are generous to the less fortunate, when you and your company contribute to causes such as homeless shelters and battered women's shelters or charities such as the Special Olympics, the Humane Society, and the American

Red Cross. Companies and leaders who show caring beyond themselves, beyond their own interests, help employees with more limited means fulfill their own desires to be generous and give back to the community. It helps them feel as if they are part of something greater than themselves, that they are part of a caring community.

For employees to feel pride in it, your gift-giving has to be commensurate with your wealth. After hurricane Katrina, some of the wealthy investment banks in New York were criticized for giving relatively small sums for victims' relief. People feel proud of their company's commitment to worthy causes only if those companies are responsibly generous. You want employees to take pride in saying, "My company contributed generously." After hurricane Katrina, our company raised thousands of dollars in employee donations, and beyond the company's own donation, Lore matched all employee contributions. The sense of pride in having helped victims of that disaster was palpable.

Encourage the Heart

When you encourage someone, you fill their heart.[2] You instill them with courage and hope. Metaphorically, when you encourage the heart you bypass the brain entirely (at least the cognitive functions!) and go straight to someone's emotional center, and what a leader wants most from people—passion, loyalty, focus, devotion—is an emotional commitment, not an intellectual commitment. It's a heart thing, not a mind thing. You accomplish it by validating people, by recognizing and praising their efforts and rewarding their triumphs.

I coached an executive years ago who said that he was having trouble with his oldest daughter, a girl of about nine. She was becoming rebellious at home and wasn't willing to try new things. He saw her changing from the bold soul she had been to a timid, cautious child. As we talked about her and his family, he revealed that he pushed her to excel, that he wanted her to be perfect. If she didn't get all A's on her report card, he scolded her and told her she could do better, that she had to be the best. I asked if he praised her for the four out of five A's she did receive, and he said no, that he didn't want her to think that anything less than perfection was okay.

The executive was in the process of crushing his daughter's spirit, so that she would grow up thinking that no matter how well she did, it would never be enough. She must have felt diminished in the eyes of one of her primary caregivers, and that feeling must have affected her self-esteem. It's no wonder she was becoming cautious. Why would she risk trying something new? The price of failure was too high for her, so the safest course was to do nothing.

Whether you are encouraging one of your children or one of your employees, the impact is the same. When you give them hope, you elevate their dreams; when you celebrate their accomplishments, you encourage them to accomplish more; and when you fill their hearts with courage, you enable them to shoot higher than they've ever shot before.

Find the Uniqueness and Beauty in Others

An essential part of making it personal is seeing others as the unique human beings they are. We have a way of distancing ourselves from others by not seeing their humanity but treating them as functions or objects instead. People are not instruments in our lives. They don't exist for our pleasure, comfort, edification, or service. They are human beings, each the center of his or her own universe—and this is true whether the person is cashiering in the company lunchroom, maintaining the company's computer network, opening a new office in China, or running your company as the CEO.

You have to see below the surface and refuse to treat people as objects—the clerk behind the desk, the bean counter, the librarian, the customer service manager, the structural engineer. Finding the beauty or uniqueness in some people is more difficult than it is in others, especially if you encounter a bitter or sour person; someone whose values, ideals, or ambitions are not aligned with your own; or someone from a group or subculture that you unconsciously are biased against. But it's always worth the effort. The surly, middle-aged woman who manages your Pasadena office may have wanted to be a doctor. The courier who's been working contentedly in your Park Avenue office for seven years may not really lack ambition; maybe he finds his fulfillment writing poetry, playing the clarinet in a jazz band, or playing semipro soccer.

The richness of humanity is that we all have our journeys, each one unique and valuable in its way. And every person has some beauty to share, something interesting about him or her, something valuable to impart. Everyone has something to teach you if you open your heart and mind to them, and it doesn't matter who you are, whether you are a hard-driving businesswoman, a macho man, a sensitive man, a spiritual person, an atheist, an engineer, a pragmatist, or a technologist. If you open yourself to the beauty and uniqueness in others, you will be immeasurably enriched and will be a better leader and manager.

A good people person takes joy in being human and sees the special qualities of each person. Great managers are also great humanitarians in that they don't view the people who work for them as resources, workers, or objects. Nor do they judge them, except in areas of performance, attitude, teamwork, and collaboration—which is what they should judge employees on. Instead, they see their employees as human beings and open themselves up to the rich diversity of the human experience. Here are some ways you can do that:

- Make the invisible people in your life visible. The bellman carrying luggage to your room, the waiter bringing you coffee, the maid cleaning your room, and the delivery person bringing the mail all have their stories to tell. So do the administrative assistants, filing clerks, accountants, sales associates, writers, technicians, drivers, interns, and others who do the work in your company. Don't pass by them day after day without notice. See, really see, them.

■ Cast a wider net. We tend to place an invisible circle around us. We allow some people inside our circle—our family and friends, trusted colleagues, special teammates, and so on. We exclude many others, including the people we don't like, don't know, don't identify with, and don't trust, but also the ones we simply don't notice, the ones who are there day by day but fade into obscurity because they aren't important to us. Cast a wider net by deliberately bringing more people into your circle and spending time with them.

■ Keep a journal and write down what's unique or beautiful about everyone who works for you. If you can't think of anything to say about someone, then you don't know them well enough. Get to know them better. They are the ones to take to lunch or chat with after work or during breaks.

■ Celebrate people's uniqueness on special occasions, or on any occasion whatsoever. Make the time to celebrate (birthdays are good, but don't wait for them).

Show People How

You make it personal by investing your time, knowledge, and experience in helping others grow. Be a teacher, a coach, and a mentor. Show others how to do things. Take an interest in helping them learn. You can send them to training programs, seminars, and workshops, but there is no substitute for individual attention and the sharing of your knowledge and experience.

Some of the finest business leaders, like Jack Welch, have considered themselves to be teachers and viewed a primary part of their role as educating others. Welch spent a considerable amount of time at Crotonville, New York, at General Electric's Leadership Development Center, meeting with managers and sharing his philosophy, leadership principles, and views about business. Partly as a consequence, GE became renowned as a company with a strong pipeline of good leaders and one of the finest leadership development systems in corporate America. Many of the leaders in Welch's pipeline have gone on to lead other companies.

Observe the Limits to Making It Personal

Can you make it too personal? Yes, if you violate cultural norms or someone's personal boundaries. Some cultures are more formal and maintain a certain amount of decorum and distance as a way of preserving those cultural norms. In some health care settings, for instance, physicians are referred to as "doctor," and in some academic settings the professors are always referred to as "professor." But in other comparable institutions even the most distinguished practitioners are called by their first names and more familiarity is encouraged. Similarly, national cultures vary in their formality and degree of familiarity in business and other organizational relationships. You need to observe the cultural norms of the environment in which you are working.

As well as cultural norms, you also need to consider people's personal boundaries. Obviously, some people are more inclined toward familiarity than others. Some people will be upset if you don't inquire about their personal lives, and some will be offended if you do. Some people like to keep their personal and business lives separate, while others fill their offices with family photos and personal mementoes, which invite people coming into their offices to comment on or ask about those personal items. People vary considerably in the extent to which they want their managers to make it personal, so there are no hard and fast rules. You have to be sensitive to each person's boundaries and be adaptable in your approach.

Even if you work in a highly informal environment where the cultural norm is to be more personal and familiar, you should still be careful about making assumptions. Some people working in that environment may nonetheless not be comfortable with too much familiarity, no matter what the cultural norm is. In some work environments, for instance, it's not uncommon for colleagues to hug one another. As I've observed them, these hugs are more collegial than affectionate, but that doesn't matter if some individuals don't like to be touched or consider hugging, especially with a manager, to be inappropriate. The key is to be sensitive to each person's boundaries, regardless of the cultural norms.

But what if you make it personal with someone—remembering their name and birthdays, taking the time to get to know them, learning some facts about their life and inquiring about them from time to time, being generous and perhaps investing in their life in appropriate ways— and they don't reciprocate? What if the person takes advantage of you or treats you disrespectfully (usually behind your back), or acts inauthentically toward you? Relationships have to be reciprocal. You can't continue to give and give if the other person never returns the gestures and gives of himself or herself as well. Customer service is a good analogy. It's important to treat customers in a friendly, warm, respectful, and courteous manner, but how long can you continue treating a customer that way if the customer is rude, belligerent, disrespectful, dishonest, and unreasonably demanding? Customers like this deserve to be fired, and so do employees. Making it personal goes both ways.

Tips for Improving Your Relationships

1. Treat employees like human beings, not human resources.

2. Remember people's names.

3. Remember people's birthdays and celebrate them.

4. Ask about people's lives and remember the facts.

5. Have one deeper level of curiosity about what someone tells you.

6. To form deeper bonds, disclose more about yourself.

7. Take time to get to know people.

8. When appropriate, invest in people's lives.

9. Be generous to the people who work for you.

10. Be generous to the less fortunate.

11. Encourage the heart.

12. Find the uniqueness and beauty in others.

13. Show people how.

14. Observe the limits to making it personal.

PART 2 | A Good Self

The way we behave reflects who we are, what we value, and what we believe. Good management stems from a good self, from the "light" side of our being. But each of us also has a shadow self. Great managers know their shadow side—and keep it in check. They are aware of the dark moods and temptations and know how to contain them. Bad managers give in to those temptations—and often ruin companies as well as lives.

The struggle with the shadow side is artfully illustrated in *Forbidden Planet.* In this film, Earth scientists explore a planet where a race of technologically advanced beings called the Krell once lived. Why the Krell vanished virtually overnight is a mystery until scientists discover one of the Krells' final inventions: a machine that makes thoughts real. The Krell were trying to imagine things into existence, but they had forgotten about "monsters from the id." Freud hypothesized that the id is the repository for our baser emotions, for the raw energy of our anger, jealousies, and fears. When the Krell made their thoughts real, the shadow emotions hidden in their ids were turned loose on their fellows, and they were all killed.

We all have a shadow side, and we must be careful not to grant it the freedom to act without the civilizing influence of the rest of our mind. Management positions can be corrupting for some people because the power and authority they are granted as managers are like the Krells' fatal invention, and when they receive that power they abuse it. Sometimes, the monsters from their id are turned loose.

In Part II, I describe the dark-side temptations and discuss how you ensure that your behavior as a manager reflects the finer aspects of your character. To maintain a good self, you need to protect your own boundaries and keep a sensible perspective—about yourself, your work, and the people you manage. You also need to keep an even keel—maintain your psychological balance. Finally, you need to avoid the various ways that you can slip into the dark side.

7 Respecting Yourself

To this point in the book, I've been talking about what your employees want. But it's also fair to ask what you want as a manager. How do you look out for yourself and your interests? How do you respect yourself?

Management positions are sought after for obvious reasons: Managers typically have more power and authority than subordinates. They sit at the locus of communication within most organizations, the seat of influence, a place from which they can exercise leadership. Managers set direction and priorities, establish or influence rewards, and have considerable control over their schedules, tasks, priorities, directions, and destiny. Managers are among the most highly compensated people in an organization and have great prestige and visibility. Management is a very attractive role for many people, especially those with high needs for power and achievement.

But management comes at a cost, sometimes a substantial cost. When you become a manager, you gain power and authority but relinquish some freedoms and must accept the burden of responsibility, a burden that routinely takes a huge toll on people. As you climb higher in the hierarchy, your greater visibility comes at the price of privacy, your behavior receives increasing scrutiny, and your decisions will often be second-guessed, certainly internally and perhaps by the media. You have to contend with impossible demands on your time, difficult people and performance problems, unattractive trade-offs, and tough decisions that must be made in an atmosphere of uncertainty and incomplete information. You may experience increasing, often ferocious stress, especially when things aren't going well, which may undermine your mental and physical health. You have less time to devote to personal interests and family (unless you are careful to safeguard these sanctuaries), and you are more exposed to the temptations that have led some leaders to defraud their companies and shareholders.

If you can take care of yourself, then managing a business unit or an organization and leading others in the pursuit of a worthwhile vision can be highly satisfying, more satisfying than just about anything else you may do in your life. But it's a big *if.* Many managers don't take care of themselves. Some become workaholics and lose the opportunity for bliss in other parts of their lives. Others devote precious years to the pursuit of success and lose their spouses or become alienated from their children. Many sacrifice their health, live badly, and die young. And many who don't suffer these calamities lose themselves in the exercise of their responsibilities and discover too late that no amount of money can fill the empty space inside or turn a tin heart to gold.

Here are some ways you can respect yourself.

Know and Respect Your Boundaries

As I've discussed, it's especially important to be vigilant about boundary violations when you are higher in a hierarchy than others, because it's easy to abuse the power of your position, intentionally or not. But you have boundaries, too. To respect yourself, you have to know where your boundaries are and ensure that other people don't violate them. You are likely to experience some boundary violations both from people above you in the management hierarchy and from the people who report to you.

Boundary Violations from Above

Unless you are the CEO, there are others above you in the organizational hierarchy, so the potential exists for boundary violations from your boss or those above your boss. The most serious boundary violations are the *ethical* ones—where a boss asks you to do something, ignore something, or cover up something that either crosses into the gray area or plunges completely into the dark side. A case in point is Thomas M. Coughlin, a former senior executive and vice chairman of Wal-Mart. In 2005 Coughlin approached a young Wal-Mart vice president, Jared Bowen, and asked him to approve $2,000 in expense payments without any receipts. Coughlin explained that the money had been used for a "union project." Bowen became uneasy about the request and notified Wal-Mart management, who launched an investigation.

They uncovered a five-year period of questionable expense payments that may have included hunting vacations, custom-made alligator boots, and a $2,590 dog pen for Coughlin's Arkansas home. According to Wal-Mart, the questionable payments may have totaled as much as $500,000. Coughlin had devoted twenty-seven years to Wal-Mart and was one of Sam Walton's old hunting buddies, so these apparent transgressions were a shock to the company. Coughlin resigned from his board seat and agreed to plead guilty to five counts of wire fraud and one count of tax evasion. As a result of the investigation, three other employees were fired as well, including Bowen.[1]

To escape this trap, you need to be aware of the temptations that can lead executives astray and avoid them. You have to be clear about your ethical boundaries and be aware of what is happening when a more senior person is asking or suggesting that you cross those boundaries. Most important, you have to refuse to be complicit in anything that you deem to be unethical or dishonest, even when this can be difficult because you believe that your livelihood or career is in jeopardy if you don't go along.

Another important boundary concerns your *self-respect.* If your boss or someone above you in the hierarchy is abusive or disrespectful toward people, you have to decide when that behavior crosses the line. And to maintain your self-respect you must be able to stand up to it. One of the most legendary abusive bosses in recent memory was "Chainsaw Al" Dunlap, former CEO of Scott Paper and then Sunbeam, who fancied himself Rambo in pinstripes. His approach to saving companies was radical cost cutting to artificially raise the stock price, and he nearly destroyed Sunbeam in the process. In her book on bad leadership, Barbara Kellerman chose Dunlap as her poster child for callous leaders. She had this to say about him: "Dunlap was an equal opportunity s.o.b., indifferent to the welfare not only of salaried employees but also of those with whom he worked directly, members of his own management team. The pressure on them was brutal, the hours exhausting, and the casualties high. He intimidated those who reported to him, and they passed that intimidation down the line." One of the executives Kellerman interviewed told her, "Dunlap created a culture of misery, an environment of moral ambiguity, indifferent to everything except the stock price. He did not lead by intellect or by vision, but by fear and intimidation. . . . The pressure was beyond tough. It was barbarous."[2]

If you have the misfortune to work for a self-styled corporate Rambo, you have to decide how much abusive behavior you will put up with—when it's directed not only toward you but also toward the people you manage. Healthy people with strong value systems have limits on what they will tolerate, no matter how much they need the job, but it can be difficult to stand up to tyrants. Abusive bosses typically bribe their followers with power, wealth, perks, or promises of greater opportunities if they remain compliant, and a number of their followers will accept the Faustian bargain and trade their self-respect for the rewards the tyrant offers. But many won't, and in today's war for executive talent, good managers don't have to remain in abusive environments. They vote with their feet and go elsewhere. If you work for an abuser, you have to decide whether the price you're paying, including loss of self-respect, is worth it.

A related boundary concerns *insensitive* but not abusive or bullying behavior. If your boss or someone senior to you in the hierarchy makes sexist, racist, or other kinds of insensitive remarks, tells off-color jokes, or otherwise behaves in ways that are unprofessional or embarrassing, you have to decide when that behavior crosses a boundary you find unacceptable. While not as intolerable as abusive or threatening behavior, this kind of insensitivity and lack of professionalism can be difficult to live with for very long.

What do you do about it? The answer depends partly on how much you trust this senior person, how open he or she is to receiving feedback or suggestions, and how good your relationship is with this person. Sometimes, you can simply change the subject—and in so doing indicate that you're uncomfortable with what the boss is saying. You can also be more direct and say, "Excuse me, but I'm uncomfortable with that joke." Or you can point out the potential negative impact of the boss's words or behavior on customers and employees or on people's perceptions of the boss and the company. Sometimes, even senior people will change their behavior when the negative effects are pointed out to them.

Two other potential boundary violations from above deserve mention. The first is what I would call the *responsibility* boundary. Sometimes, senior people force subordinates to do what the senior person ought to do. I've seen cases, for instance, when a senior person—because he was a conflict avoider—ordered a subordinate manager to fire someone the subordinate manager did not think should be fired or to deal with a situation the subordinate manager really didn't have the authority to deal with. When a senior person avoids taking responsibility, you may need to say, "John, this is something I really think you should handle," or "John, I think the people involved really need to hear from you."

Finally, people senior to you may violate a *privacy* boundary by asking about, commenting on, or otherwise intruding on your personal life in ways that are uncomfortable for you. The most egregious case I've ever seen was a boss who insisted that a junior manager's spouse host a party for visiting clients because this spouse was such a good hostess. The junior manager felt (rightly) that this was a violation of his privacy and an intrusion into his personal life but didn't feel he could say no. He and his wife soon left the company rather than confront the issue, and the company lost a good high-potential leader. Boundary violations like this also occur when bosses insist that managers below them in the hierarchy make repeated and unreasonable personal sacrifices (such as canceling family vacations at the last moment). Of course, sacrifices must be made now and then, but some senior people take advantage of a junior person's willingness to sacrifice for the sake of the business and demand too much, too often. Give them an inch, and they take a mile. At some point, you have to say no.

Boundary Violations from Below

Although generally not as difficult as boundary violations from above, boundary violations can also come from the people who report to you. Employees are also sometimes guilty of violating *responsibility boundaries.* They will refuse to make the decisions they should make, ask you what they should do, and then blame you if something goes wrong. Risk-averse employees are often very good at delegating up, and the clever ones can do it so subtly that you don't know it's been done.

Coaching is usually a good short-term strategy for handling upward delegators. If they persist, however, you may need to let them go.

If you are good-natured, friendly, and supportive (as I've suggested you should be), then another boundary violation can come from employees who take advantage of your good nature. Let's call it the *good-nature boundary.* These are the employees who, seeing that you are generous in allowing time off during the workday for things such as dental appointments, start taking more time off than necessary for personal errands. Or they'll prevail upon their good relationship with you by asking for personal favors you can't bestow on everyone. Or they'll start conducting more personal business at work than they should and expect you to allow it because they work so hard at other times. The list goes on. Good-natured bosses are often taken advantage of. The solution isn't to be a jerk. It's to be clear with employees and yourself about the boundaries and be gentle but firm when those boundaries are crossed.

The *work-life balance boundary* can come from below but is as likely to come from you. If you are a high-achieving manager, you may also drive yourself excessively hard and be self-sacrificing to the extreme. The worst case I've ever encountered was a thirtysomething professional woman who worked for a prestigious management consulting firm. The firm encouraged her in subtle and not-so-subtle ways to work extraordinarily long hours, and she was driven by her own zeal for professional success. Four years before I met her, she had given birth to a daughter, and she and her husband, who was also a hard-driving professional, had hired a nanny to look after their daughter. During a coaching session with this young woman, she told me that her daughter, whom she rarely saw, did not know that she was her mother. It would be hard to overstate the extent of this tragedy, certainly for the parents but especially for the child. When you cross the work-life balance boundary, you usually damage more than just your own life.

Know How to Say No

You need to be able to say no even when your boundaries aren't being violated. Sometimes, you just have to protect yourself (and your sanity) by saying no to requests or demands on your time. It's not easy, especially when you are the type of person who tries to please others and when you are driven to excel at everything you do.

Some managers have the caretaker syndrome. Whenever needs arise—from customers, superiors, peers, or employees—caretakers will do what it takes to meet those needs. Caretakers apply liberal doses of time and talent to every problem, and because they're willing to work so hard, they are usually successful. It's how they rose to their current positions (or at least this is what they believe), and they think that to continue succeeding they have to do whatever it takes, despite the cost to themselves and their families.

Caretakers not only don't know how to say no, they often think that no is not acceptable. The people they work with sense this and learn that they can give any problem to the caretaker, and he or she will handle it. For the caretaker, the reward for working hard and doing well is to work harder and do even more. The caretakers I've known are frequently drained and may burn out prematurely in their careers because they never learn how to say no. Moreover, many of them become resentful of other people who can and do say no. The solution is at once simple but difficult: you have to know your boundaries and protect them, and this means setting priorities in your work and life and not allowing other people or circumstances to dissuade you from keeping your priorities straight.

Here are some ways to say no:

■ If you sense that you're being pressured to say yes, delay your response to give yourself time to reflect on what you really want to agree to. Just say, "I need to think about it. Ask me again tomorrow morning." Then, when you're away from the person and the immediate pressure, think about what you want and prepare your response.

▪ Ask for or suggest alternatives: "Who else could help you with this? What options do you have?" When you engage the other person in problem solving, you often both see alternatives that the other person hadn't considered and that are preferable to your saying yes.

▪ Say no but offer to help find another solution: "I don't have time to help you with that, but you might ask John." It's often easier to say no if you feel like you're still being helpful.

▪ Appeal to the other person's sense of balance: "Mary, I'd really like to help you with that, but I promised myself I'd go skiing this weekend. I'm trying to get some work-life balance and need to protect that time. I'm sure you understand." When you appeal to someone's values, they are often reluctant to press you on something they've asked for. Obviously, it depends on the situation, but values appeals frequently succeed where logical arguments fail.

▪ Practice saying no. Start with small things. Practice saying no to the less consequential matters in your life and progress to the more consequential ones as you gain comfort saying no. This is a form of self-therapy, and it takes time, but it will work. I've used it with some coaching clients, and it's helped them tremendously.

▪ Be clear about your priorities and draw a line in the sand on the things you will and will not do. Sometimes, it helps to say no if you've done some clear thinking about what's important and what you'll agree to or not before people make requests.

▪ Just say no. This is very difficult for some people. It may feel uncomfortable at first, but with practice you'll become an expert at it.

Set Aside Time for Yourself

Management roles can be demanding, challenging, stressful, and exhausting—but also extremely fulfilling, personally and professionally. Because it can be so fulfilling, many people I've coached throw themselves into the role, sometimes to the exclusion of other parts of their lives. As a number of other authors have observed, it's important to set aside time for yourself, to stop and smell the roses. To truly respect yourself, you have to manage your heart and soul. Type A personalities can burn themselves out. The most tragic ones work themselves to an early death and, because they saved no time for themselves, never savor the richness of life that was possible for them.

Nurture Yourself

To nurture your spirit, you have to know what is nourishing, and the source of nourishment for you is your dreams. Nurture yourself, whatever form that takes. Years ago in graduate school, I took an acting class from an outstanding instructor who gave every ounce of her energy to her students every week. Then we went to class one week and she said, "I've been giving and giving and giving. Today, I need you to give to me." So we spent the next hour entertaining her—telling her stories, dancing for her, singing, and so on. It was an unusual class, to say the least. But I learned something very important, which is that when you are in charge you can't constantly give to others without now and then receiving back. Whatever else she taught me about acting, I learned an important lesson about the need to look after yourself and to insist on being nourished from time to time instead of just doing the nourishing.

As you reflect on this, ask yourself these questions:

1. **What are the ten to twenty things you'd like to do before you die?** Someone remarked once that this is a gruesome question, that we shouldn't be thinking about death. My response was that since death is inevitable, is it better to die fulfilled and enriched, or unfulfilled and impoverished in spirit? Instead of a like-to-do list, make it a must-do list. And instead of hoping these things will happen someday, take charge of your life and make them happen, one at a time, starting now, or next week, or next month, but not "someday."

2. **If you didn't have to work, what would you do with your time? What would be fulfilling for you?** I recommend that people think outside the job. The people I've coached have mentioned diving on shipwrecks, opening a small bakery, writing poetry, trekking around the world, climbing the seven summits, spending more time with grandchildren, volunteering at a hospice, and lying on a beach and reading more books. Your dreams nourish your spirit. Dream large and then go for it. You may be busy, but respect yourself by making the time.

3. **Besides your job or profession, what makes you happy?** What do you find nourishing? Engaging? Exhilarating? If you could take a night school class in something, what would it be? If you could take a summer off and go somewhere else in the world, where would you go? What would you do?

Ensure That You Are Recognized, Too

Even though as managers we may be happy with the compensation, perks, prestige, power, visibility, and opportunities we get, most of us still crave the occasional pat on the back for a job well done. Some organizations and senior leaders are good about recognizing outstanding contributions and performance from members of the management team, but others aren't. It's not unusual for high-performing managers to feel unappreciated, despite the tangible rewards of success, and, like everyone else who works hard and feels unrecognized for that hard work, when you feel unappreciated you can become resentful and surly. You are human, and you need attaboys or attagirls, too.

The best way to ensure that you are appreciated is to create a high-recognition environment by showing appreciation for others. When employees feel appreciated, they are more likely to show appreciation. Conversely, if they perceive that the boss is unappreciative, they will withhold their applause. Here are some other ways to elicit appreciation:

- Let people know what you've accomplished. It's best to share it as news rather than as self-promotion, and the news should be about what the company has done or what a particular initiative just achieved. Sensible people are rightly wary of anything that sounds like self-promotion, so it should not be, or appear to be, self-aggrandizing. But they appreciate hearing news and will often respond to the news by sending congratulations and acknowledgments for those who were responsible for the success.

- Forward accolades received from customers. Everyone likes to know when you or the company received an appreciation from a customer, and often the best recognition you can get is the pride you feel in having led the initiative that customers appreciated. Generally, however, people will acknowledge the accolade from the customer and send their congratulations.

- When you have accomplished something noteworthy, you should let people outside the company know about it through your marketing or public relations groups. It helps build recognition for the company and reflects positively on you.

▓ Share the good news at home. Your spouse or significant other, children, and friends are likely to show appreciation if you let them know when you've had a success at work. For many people, this type of recognition is best. Of course, you must celebrate their triumphs as well.

▓ Celebrate your wins yourself. Whether or not recognition comes from others, when you deserve a pat on the back, treat yourself to a weekend away, a game of golf, a bottle of champagne, or whatever would be a fitting celebration for you. And, no, it's not tacky for you to celebrate yourself.

Some managers I've coached have been wary about seeking recognition for themselves, although they acknowledge that when it comes they enjoy it. Most of us have learned to avoid anything that seems like self-promotion or self-aggrandizement, and while self-aggrandizement can be carried to excess, there is nothing wrong with sharing the news of your or your company's accomplishments and wanting a well-deserved pat on the back for successes and triumphs.

Make Your Needs and Expectations Known

In order for you to get your needs met, you have to make your needs and expectations known. One of the executives I work with has a spouse who doesn't remember her birthday or their anniversary. Rather than be upset about this, she finds subtle ways to remind him. I've worked with a number of managers who are good about making business needs and expectations clear to everyone they work with but who don't make their personal needs and expectations known. Then they resent it when people can't read their minds. Whether it's business or personal, don't expect people to intuit your needs and expectations. You respect yourself by making your needs clear.

Trust Your Instincts

You respect yourself by trusting your instincts, which can be difficult in a world where rational analysis and reasoned arguments prevail. However, as Malcolm Gladwell points out, "there are moments, particularly in times of stress, when haste does not make waste, when our snap judgments and first impressions can offer a much better means of making sense of the world. . . . Decisions made very quickly can be every bit as good as decisions made cautiously and deliberately."[3] If it feels right in your gut, it's probably right, and if it feels wrong, it's probably wrong. But we sometimes can't articulate why we feel the way we do, and that hamstrings some managers I've known. They long for proof that reduces the decision risk, so they learn over time not to trust themselves and their instincts. That's a mistake.

Respecting yourself means respecting your instincts, trusting that you know more than you think you know, having faith in your experience and capabilities, and putting your self-doubts to rest.

Make It Okay to Change Your Mind

I've met managers who felt that once they made a decision they were bound to stick with it or appear wishy-washy or indecisive. Robert Cialdini notes that people have an almost obsessive desire to be consistent with what they have already said or done: "Once we have made a choice or taken a stand, we will encounter personal and interpersonal pressures to behave consistently with that commitment. Those pressures will cause us to respond in ways that justify our earlier decision."[4]

Of course, some people will use your tendency to be consistent with your commitments against you if you try to change your mind and reverse an earlier decision. But it's not a sign of weakness to change your mind if later information indicates that your initial commitment or decision was not optimal. You want to keep your commitments, of course, but there is no dishonor in changing your mind if doing so will enable you to make a better decision. Rather than being a sign of weakness, changing your mind can be a sign of growth and flexibility. Moreover, reversing an earlier decision made in error is a sign of strength and honesty.

Believe in Yourself

In my experience, not all managers are self-assured and confident. I've met numerous managers who were plagued by uncertainties, weren't sure if they were doing well or doing all they should, and lacked confidence in important areas. Sometimes, they were hampered by performance anxiety (public speaking being the number one fear), and sometimes they weren't sure how to deal with tough human issues (including dealing with difficult bosses). I've offered the following advice to managers who in one way or another didn't believe in themselves:

▪ Assert yourself appropriately. Don't be aggressive, but if you have a clear point of view about something, express it boldly and confidently (which is often easier said than done). When asserting yourself, ask supporting questions such as "How do you see it?" or "What alternatives do we have?" or "What other approach would give us trade-offs this favorable?" Be sure to listen carefully and be assertive but not intransigent about your point. Listen, adapt, collaborate.

▪ Don't accept responsibility for others' misfortunes. Some managers I've known have taken on too much social responsibility. They felt it was up to them to make everyone's lives right, and they wound up neglecting their own needs as a consequence.

■ Don't shoulder more blame than you deserve. Some managers accept the blame for things they clearly weren't responsible for. Sometimes, they say that they are to blame because they should have done more or foreseen some pitfalls or been somewhere when they had to be somewhere else. You should accept the responsibility for the things you are responsible for, but you don't have to carry all of the burden. Some people will gladly allow you to accept the blame if it means the spotlight won't be turned on them, and others cope with failure by finding someone else to blame for it. You shouldn't be a patsy for people, especially peers or superiors, who are seeking someone to victimize.

Act Self-Confidently but Allow Yourself to Be Wrong Now and Then

I've encountered many good people who lacked confidence in themselves and behaved as though they were waiting to be corrected. They often drove themselves well beyond what is humanly possible (or expected by others), and they sometimes forced others to work too much, too long, and too hard. You need to reach a point where you no longer have to prove yourself. If you don't, you will run over people, drive them to exhaustion or burnout, make everyone miserable, or demand so much that others lose their self-confidence and commitment to the enterprise.

The healthiest approach is to believe in yourself, act confidently but not stubbornly, allow yourself to make mistakes, learn from those mistakes, and lead others boldly but with equal doses of humanity, forgiveness, and challenge.

Follow Your Bliss

You will be happiest in life if you pursue your passions, if you do what you love doing. It makes you a happier, more interesting, more vibrant, more engaging person. Conversely, if you spend your days, months, and years doing what you hate, you will likely be unhappy, depressed, morose, tedious, cranky, and unfit to be in others' company.

Joseph Campbell advised his students to "follow your bliss," and that is good advice. Remember that what is blissful for one person may be tedious and horrifying to another. That's what makes the world interesting. I've met managers whose nirvana was running the paint department in a large hardware store and others who loved being district sales manager for a pharmaceutical company but whose real passion was black-and-white nature photography on weekends. It really doesn't matter as long as you know what makes you happy.

Tips for Improving Your Relationships

1. Know and respect your boundaries. (Beware of boundary violations from above and from below.)

2. Know how to say no.

3. Set aside time for yourself.

4. Nurture yourself.

5. Ensure that you are recognized, too.

6. Make your needs and expectations known.

7. Trust your instincts.

8. Make it okay to change your mind.

9. Believe in yourself.

10. Act self-confidently but allow yourself to be wrong now and then.

11. Follow your bliss.

8 Keeping an Even Keel

G ary was an executive who had a problem with losing his temper. He didn't just lose it; he lost it badly. Before even becoming aware that he was angry, he'd be shouting at people and
cursing—which he otherwise rarely did—alienating employees to the
point that people were no longer willing to give him bad news. Later,
he'd realize how big a mess he'd made of things and would feel contrite
and ashamed of his behavior. But by then it was too late.

When I asked Gary why he became so angry, he used what I call the
"Geraldine defense," after the character comedian Flip Wilson made
famous on the 1960s TV show *Rowan and Martin's Laugh-In*. Geraldine
was a bawdy older woman who constantly misbehaved. When caught,
she would deflect responsibility for her wrongdoing by saying, "The
devil made me do it!" That's essentially what Gary told me: if only
someone hadn't done this or that, if only some event hadn't happened,
or if only something hadn't taken place when it did, he wouldn't have
lost it. He had a thousand reasons why everything and everyone else was
responsible for his bad behavior. Working with him was primarily a
matter of getting him to recognize and accept that although other people's

actions might trigger his outbursts, he was responsible for the outbursts, not others.

Once Gary realized that the only person responsible for his reactions was he himself, he could work on the hard part—what he could do about it. Gary is one of those people who have poor impulse control. As in *ready, fire, aim,* they act before thinking and are often unaware that they're angry until well after they are venting their anger. They react instantaneously to situations and are deep into a disaster before they recognize the need for disaster control. Other people may have good impulse control but still find themselves being thrown off center by upsetting people or unexpected events. They can be thrown off balance in stressful situations and act or react in ways that are normally uncharacteristic of them.

Emotionally intelligent people know their triggers and watch for them. When they sense those triggers being pulled, they manage their reactions and avoid the automatic behaviors that can exacerbate the situation. The key is to stay centered when something happens that would ordinarily lead to you lose your temper or your emotional balance.

Here are some ways you can keep on an even keel.

Find a Discipline That Helps You Achieve Inner Peace

I learned about staying centered from the Japanese martial art aikido, which could be described as a method of coordinating your actions, intentions, and emotions. Much of the art of aikido lies in keeping yourself centered or balanced and redirecting your opponent's energy away from you. Aikido has been called the art of peace because its intent is not to harm others but to channel their aggression away from you into a beneficial resolution. In an aikido dojo, you learn to breathe deeply, relax progressively, and locate your center low in your midsection (the higher your center, the more off balance you can become). You also learn to remain calm and deliberate in the face of aggression. Of course, most of us in business never face outright physical aggression, but it helps to remain centered when we are dealing with product failures, manufacturing delays, quality shortfalls, lost contracts or bids, disgruntled clients, employees in conflict, upsetting market news, tough competitors, adverse media coverage, and other common business challenges.

Other avenues to learning how to stay centered include prayer, yoga, meditation, relaxation, deep breathing, music, reading, hypnosis, imaging, massage, biofeedback, and therapy. People also find this sense of inner peace through hiking, mountain climbing, river rafting, bicycling, and other sports and through painting, pottery making, sculpture, and other forms of art. It would be fair to say that people the world over spend billions of dollars and countless hours in the pursuit of calmness, enlightenment, and peace. Whatever you call it, and whatever avenue you take, the goal is to find yourself and your center and to learn to maintain yourself in the blur of modern life, and this includes keeping an even keel while interacting with other people.

Stay Centered

Find what works for you: counting to ten, taking a deep breath, progressively relaxing parts of your body, taking a sixty-second nap, getting a massage, applying gentle pressure to your pressure points, lowering your center, and so on. There are no magic bullets, only what works for you, and you need to discover what that is. If you are someone who tends to lose your temper when provocative circumstances occur, then you need to discover what helps you remain centered and practice it.

For me, the answer has been to keep things in perspective and not agonize over past mistakes. When something happens, it happens. Accept it and move on. Figure out how to solve the problem or rectify the situation, and get on with it. Of course, some calamities are greater than others, and it's sometimes difficult not to become upset, especially when you've worked hard on something, invested a lot of heart and soul in it, and then seen it destroyed or diminished by incompetence or bad luck. Still, once the disaster has happened, it is what it is. At that point, the best you can do is clean up the mess and figure out where to go from there. This attitude has had a wonderfully calming effect on me, and I've found it much easier to remain centered when I look at circumstances this way.

For me, it's essential to have a healthy perspective on what matters, and ultimately it isn't what you own or how many awards are on your walls; it's how you've lived your life and what relationships you have. The most successful people I've known value the company of others and have the capacity to relax and remain centered, even if they are intense and driven when they choose to be.

Know Your Triggers—and Control Your Reactions to Them

You need to know what triggers an automatic emotional reaction in you. In my years of coaching, I've asked many managers what triggers them, and here are some of the things I've heard:

- The implication that I've got the facts wrong
- An accusation or suggestion that I am dishonest or lack integrity
- The suggestion that I've been too hasty in making a decision and haven't considered all the facts
- Members of my staff trying to position themselves by backstabbing a peer

■ Someone calling a meeting and not having a clear, concise agenda

■ Employees failing to complete an assignment and then saying after the fact that they didn't have enough information (They should've asked up front!)

You probably know what your triggers are, but if you aren't sure, it's worth taking a few moments to reflect on what happens and writing it down. What makes you angry, annoyed, or irritable? What causes an emotional reaction in you? What gets you off balance? The first step in controlling your reactions is to recognize that you are irritated or upset and then discover why. What prompted it? What happened to set you off?

You need to develop sufficient awareness of your triggers so that when they are pulled in the future you aren't automatically hijacked by your reactions. Of course, this is easier said than done. The truth is that many of us get knocked off center when things get dicey, and it's difficult to catch yourself at the point where you begin to lose your balance. Nonetheless, with enough awareness and practice, it is possible to sensitize yourself so that when your triggers are pulled you become aware of it. The key is to know what situations or people are likely to be provocative to you and prepare yourself before encountering them. Also, many of us can feel a kind of warmth emanating from within when we are becoming angry or upset. If you sense that feeling, you should be aware that something has triggered you and you're likely to be knocked off center unless you control your reactions. However you do it, the art to keeping an even keel, in life as in sailing, is to sense when a strong wind has started to blow and adjust your sails accordingly.

Finally, don't blame others for your feelings and reactions. A strong wind may start to blow your boat over, but how you handle a strong wind is your responsibility. It's natural for us to want to place the blame for our anger and angry reactions elsewhere. It's easier if the problem is "out there" rather than "in here." It lets you off the hook and protects your self-image, but as long as you attribute the problem to others, you have no reason to change, and these triggers, like a strong wind over the water, will continue to blow you off center.

Be Proud, but Not Vain, about Your Accomplishments

I've coached hundreds of executives who believed that only they could have pulled off a major coup—whether it was completing a difficult merger, developing a new client or managing a client-from-hell relationship, conducting a tough negotiation, or bringing a particular product to market. With rare exceptions, this is not true, but the idea that "only I could have done it" is common. I don't mean that you shouldn't be proud of what you've accomplished. You should. But keep things in perspective. There is a natural progression from pride to vanity, from there to arrogance and narcissism, and from there to entitlement and other dangerous places along the road to the dark side.

Keeping an even keel means having a healthy perspective about yourself and your accomplishments. It's laudable to be ambitious and achievement oriented, but not at others' expense or at your own loss of humility. Healthy pride is not relational—it doesn't depend on being better than others. Healthy pride is about achieving your potential, whatever that may be, and about feeling good about yourself. It's about doing the best you can do. Psychologist Abraham Maslow referred to these drives as *self-esteem* and *self-actualization*—the two highest levels in his hierarchy of needs. Healthy pride means having high self-esteem and realizing your full potential, becoming what you were born to become, whatever that may be; this is what people typically strive for when their more basic needs (physiological, safety, and social) have been met.

Be Resilient

When it is battered by powerful winds, a resilient tree bends but does not break and returns to its former position when the winds stop. Like that tree, as a manager you need to model resilience and show others how to accept misfortune with grace and then make the best of whatever the new circumstances are. One of the more memorable leaders I've ever known led a business unit that faced an unprecedented disaster when the Arab oil embargo in the early 1970s wiped out more than 70 percent of its market overnight. Facing a depressed, even desperate group of employees, he said, "What an incredible opportunity we now have." With that simple declaration, he transformed their mood from despair to determination, and they set about remaking themselves and their services. It was a struggle, but they prevailed.

Diane Coutu notes that resilient people share three characteristics: "an ability to face reality as it is, not as one thinks or wishes it should be; deeply rooted beliefs, sometimes reinforced by well-articulated values, that sustain a conviction that life has meaning; and the capacity to improvise with whatever is at hand, in particular to call on resources within oneself in unique and creative ways."[1] Resilient people are adaptive and resourceful, but most of all they are optimistic. They believe that misfortune is inevitable but defeat is not. Furthermore, they have what psychologists refer to as an *internal locus of control.* They believe that their fate is in their hands, that they have the power to influence their destiny. Clearly, resilience is critical in maintaining an even keel.

Receive Feedback Graciously

Everyone savors positive feedback. We all want to hear how well we've done and how much people like us, but most people bridle at negative feedback. Many resist hearing it and become defensive, and a few people find it so disturbing that they attack the messenger.

For a host of reasons, receiving feedback can be challenging. Feedback is sometimes not about how you've performed but about who you are. You were probably doing your best, so hearing that someone didn't like what you did can be painful. You may have reached a point in your life where you feel enough is enough. For us middle-aged, successful professionals and managers, *still* to be getting negative feedback can feel like all the hard work we've done to get where we are hasn't made us immune from criticism. It can be especially difficult to hear negative feedback if the person giving it is someone we don't trust, don't respect, don't find credible, or don't like. And many people aren't skilled at giving feedback. They're judgmental, make sweeping generalizations, or use a condemnatory tone, and their lack of skill can make hearing the feedback even more difficult. Finally, it can be as difficult for an older person to hear feedback from someone much younger as it is for the younger person to give it.

Nonetheless, it's important that you receive feedback graciously, no matter what the source or how disconcerting the feedback might be. If you are in a management role, it's crucial that you be a role model for giving and receiving feedback in a thoughtful, timely, gracious, and competent manner. You can't expect others to do what you are unwilling or unable to do yourself, and your willingness to receive feedback largely establishes the extent to which your group will have a culture of learning and development. If you do not accept feedback graciously, you send the signal that you don't want to hear it, that feedback is not welcome, and, in the worst of cases, that you'll defend yourself if you perceive that you are being attacked. It shuts down communication, inhibits people from telling you some things you may need to hear, and creates an unhealthy double standard if you expect your employees to listen to your feedback when you won't listen to theirs.

The key to receiving feedback graciously is to think of any feedback, from *any* source, as someone's impression, not as reality. Feedback is perception, not truth, and this holds for positive as well as negative feedback. Praise is wonderful to hear, and you should feel good about it, but it's not the truth about you. It's just someone's perception. Negative feedback is sometimes difficult to hear, and you should listen to it and learn from it, but it's also not the truth about you. It's just someone's perception.

When I hear negative feedback from someone, I try to understand how the person might have formed that impression. Sometimes, I see that I could have said or done something differently. I may not have intended to create the impression that person got, so it's useful to know that he or she reacted differently than I expected. Maybe I can do it differently next time and avoid that same misperception. Sometimes, someone didn't like or appreciate something I said or did, but I would not have done it differently and wouldn't change a thing. Still, it's useful to know how I came across. That's why I said earlier that in terms of performance feedback there really is no bad news.

To accept feedback graciously, you should try to do two things. First, be sure you understand what the person has told you. If something is unclear, ask for clarification. Asking clarifying questions shows that you are taking the feedback seriously and are interested in the person's point of view. Even when you think you understood what the person said, it's usually helpful to restate it: "So what you're saying is . . ." At least some of the time, you'll be surprised to discover that you did not hear it correctly, which is useful to know before you respond.

Second, always thank the person for the feedback. If it was difficult for you to hear, it was probably difficult for the other person to give. People have to extend themselves to give feedback. Most of the time, they don't have to give it to you and they give it in the spirit of trying to be helpful, so the courteous and gracious thing to do is express your appreciation.

Allow Others to Be Right

One executive I worked with would never admit that she had made a mistake, was in error, or might not have had the best ideas. She would defend her positions to an absurd extreme, even when history showed them to be glaringly, stupendously wrong. She would give an order and later reverse it when the outcome wasn't what she expected—and then blame her subordinates for doing the wrong thing. When someone said, "But that's what you told us to do," she would claim that they hadn't understood her.

Having to be right about everything places an unreasonable burden on you. It inhibits your ability to listen, discover, learn, and grow, and it can make you unreasonably contentious with the people who work for you. To keep an even keel, you need to allow others to be right and yourself to be wrong. Encourage ideas from others, give credit where credit is due, and acknowledge—to yourself and others—when you've made a mistake. When you allow someone else to be right, you encourage that person's heart; when you allow yourself to be wrong, you give yourself the gifts of forgiveness and understanding.

Don't Run Hot and Cold

I worked with a manager some years ago whom I'll call Catherine. One minute she would be friendly and personable; the next minute she'd be cold and distant. I could never uncover the reason for her mood swings. As nearly as I could determine, nothing happened to cause her to run hot one moment and cold the next. You can imagine how disconcerting it was to work with her. You never knew what to expect: happy, sad, funny, irrational, helpful, pessimistic, warm, angry, caring, spiteful. She expressed the full range of human emotions and seemed to flit randomly from one extreme to another.

I think Catherine may have been manic-depressive, which would have accounted for her unpredictable mood swings, but I've known many other executives who appeared to be psychologically healthy but nonetheless were moody and sometimes unpredictable in their behavior. We all have bad days, but if you're in a leadership role your bad days can have an amplified effect if employees interpret your moodiness as disdain, disaffection, or disapproval. It may be difficult to lift yourself, by force of will, out of a bad mood, but you can at least acknowledge that you're in a bad mood and apologize if you run roughshod over somebody. The key is to have enough self-awareness to know that you're in a foul mood, which is difficult for some people. Then take care not to allow your mood to infect others. Be aware of what you're doing and saying. It may not be possible to affect a good mood if you're feeling poorly—and that probably wouldn't seem genuine anyway. But it's important to manage your interactions with people so your occasional foul moods don't affect them. If you tend to run radically hot and cold—beyond occasional moodiness—then you may have a more serious issue and should see a physician or counselor.

Allow Yourself to Be Human

The opposite of the person who runs hot and cold is the person who is unnaturally even tempered all the time. They try to be the perfect consultant or the perfect manager or the perfect mom or dad. Karen was this kind of manager. She was one of the few women at the time I knew her to have reached a fairly senior leadership position in her firm. She was also raising a family (two daughters and a son), volunteering in her community, trying to hold a marriage together, and dealing with ailing parents while proving to herself and her colleagues that she deserved to be in the management role she was in and leading a very challenging unit that had been underperforming when she was given the role. It appeared to almost everyone around her that she was always bright, energetic, focused, and in command, but her superwoman facade was beginning to show some cracks, and she confided in me that she was on the verge of seriously losing her mind.

The problem, she realized, was that she was allowing her own and everyone else's high expectations of her to shape the persona she felt compelled to project, no matter what she actually felt. She was terrified of doing a poor job at work, partly because she believed it would reflect badly on *all* women, and she felt that she was single-handedly responsible for holding it all together—her marriage, her children, her parents' lives, her volunteer work. To everyone around her, she projected a calm, capable, happy veneer. Inside, she felt anxious, angry, frustrated, and increasingly stretched to impossible dimensions, and she didn't want anyone to know how close to the brink she was. It was particularly important to her that she not let her family know that she wasn't all right. As a coach, I suggested to her that she needed to allow herself to be human.

It's okay to feel bad sometimes. It's okay to have aches and pains and to fret over life's problems. It's okay to be overwhelmed and to acknowledge that you're stressed. It's okay to take time off and to devote time to yourself. It's okay to not like part of the job. It's okay to be imperfect. It's okay to be angry now and then (so long as you manage it, not take it out unreasonably on others, and learn from it).

Something I've learned is that our emotions are okay. They are sending a message. When you're frustrated, upset, or angry, your body is telling you something useful. The best you can do is to strive to understand that message and learn from it. What's making you angry? What is the source of the frustration? Why does this frustrate you? What does that tell you about what you need and how you respond to circumstances?

My friend Paul Krauss, who is a retired director of a management consulting firm, once observed that the people who got ahead in his firm were not the robotic, perfect Ivy League graduates who had no apparent flaws but instead were the people who had hairs out of place, got soup on their ties, wore wrinkled clothes now and then, and were willing to be resolutely themselves, whatever that was. Why is this true? Because they didn't have a false image to defend. They allowed themselves to be human in front of their colleagues and clients. They were genuine, so other people felt more comfortable in their presence. The fact is that we are suspicious of people who seem too good, too unshakeable, too perfect. "Doesn't anything ever faze that guy?" we might ask. We feel more comfortable with people who have flaws, just like us. It's their humanity that we recognize, accept, and respect.

So what does this have to do with keeping an even keel? The answer is that you can't stay centered if you don't know where your center is. If you are projecting a false image to yourself and others, you have to work too hard to maintain the facade. You will lose touch with how you really feel and who you really are, and you will get knocked off center through the very act of trying to be flawlessly centered. You aren't a robot so you shouldn't try to act like one. Allow yourself to be human.

Have a Sense of Humor about Yourself

You keep an even keel by being able to laugh at yourself. If you're too serious about you, it's easy to be knocked off center by a mistake, embarrassment, slip of the tongue, or spilled cup of coffee. Occasionally, you need to trip on a banana peel and pick yourself up laughing at the fool you've just made of yourself. If you can do that, you'll be less stressed, more self-accepting, and happier about your occasionally clumsy self.

I was on an airplane once with an executive who was flying to Chicago for an important business meeting. It was a one-day trip for him, and he was wearing a nice business suit with a white shirt and silk tie. During the trip, one of the flight attendants spilled a cup of orange juice all over the front of his suit. Had this happened to some executives I've known, they would have become irate, screamed at the flight attendant, demanded an apology, and threatened to sue the airline unless the person bought them new clothing. However, this fellow took it in stride. The flight attendant was mortified, and he did his best to reassure her, saying it was just an accident. As he dried his newly orange-stained white shirt with a towel, I asked if he would need to buy a new shirt and suit before his meeting. "No," he said, chuckling. "I won't have time. Besides, this will make a good story." The lesson he taught me is that 90 percent of keeping an even keel is attitude and perspective.

Tips for Improving Your Relationships

1. Find a discipline that helps you achieve inner peace.

2. Stay centered.

3. Know your triggers—and control your reactions to them.

4. Be proud, but not vain, about your accomplishments.

5. Be resilient.

6. Receive feedback graciously.

7. Allow others to be right.

8. Don't run hot and cold.

9. Allow yourself to be human.

10. Have a sense of humor about yourself.

9

Behaving Badly
(and How to Avoid It)

Bosses who become seriously imbalanced and tip over into the dark side of leadership—managers who are insensitive and cruel, demanding and petty, suspicious, conniving, and mean— are truly toxic. In this chapter I describe the different types of dark side leadership and then talk about how to avoid these kinds of behaviors.

Many kinds of toxic bosses are out there. A few of them—including "Chainsaw Al" Dunlap, who considered himself "Rambo in pinstripes," and Leona Helmsley, the so-called Queen of Mean—are legendary for their bad behavior. These petty dictators leave a trail of broken bodies and careers in their wake, run corporations into the ground, or so alienate those around them that talented people bail out in record numbers as the stock price plummets. It's difficult to understand why these toxic bosses aren't more aware of the impact of their behavior, especially when things start going badly. Perhaps they are insulated by their monumental egos and just don't see the carpet of destruction they leave behind them.

Understanding the Dark Side of Leadership

In the 1990s, Bill Doherty and I developed a five-part leadership model that sought to describe every instance of effective leadership. In creating this model, we read dozens of books on leadership and reviewed numerous existing leadership models. Our goal was to identify what effective leaders did that made them effective, and we identified about one hundred distinct leadership competencies or behaviors. Subsequent validity studies on our model showed that these behaviors clustered into five areas, which we labeled moral, intellectual, collaborative, courageous, and visionary/inspirational leadership (see figure below).

The leadership model we developed is useful, particularly for helping executives assess their strengths and developmental needs as leaders, but it proved to be less useful in helping executives discern where and why they might derail, and we could not use it to diagnose such leadership catastrophes as the Enron collapse, the executive fraud at WorldCom, or the many other cases of executive malfeasance that have occurred in recent years. In short, our model was a "light side" or positive model of leadership that ignored the dark side. To create a more comprehensive picture of leadership, we undertook further research on how managers go wrong. We focused on private equity firms whose partners had considerable experience with portfolio companies and their executive teams. The partners helped us understand what happens when their portfolio companies do not perform well. In particular, they helped us identify typical ways in which the executives of the less-successful companies behaved that reduced their effectiveness and negatively affected the performance of their companies.

We call this the dark side model. It includes eighteen types of dark-side leadership, which also cluster into five areas: Periscopes, Lone Wolves, Deceivers, Bridge Burners, and the Great Leader. To develop effective relationships with your employees, it's important that you be aware of these dark side archetypes and know whether you may be in danger of falling into one of them.

The Periscope Leader Types

Periscope leaders have limited self-awareness. They are too narrowly focused on one thing and can't see the broader picture.

The Mr. or Ms. Nice Guy

Mr. or Ms. Nice Guy leaders are excessively benevolent. Although benevolence is normally a virtue, managers who are excessively benevolent are too nice and may have difficulty making tough business and people decisions. Furthermore, they may avoid conflict and not like to challenge others or make waves. They usually set a positive tone for the quality of interpersonal relationships in the group or organization, but they are often too positive and can't balance this with the need to be decisive, tough, and candid when necessary.

If you are trying too hard to keep all your employees happy, you risk being too generous and not critical or candid enough. You may be too trusting of others, too generous with rewards and recognition, and too anxious to avoid conflict because you hate strife. A positive tone and an enriching and satisfying working environment are important, but you also have to set high standards and hold people accountable for their work.

The My Way or the Highway

My Way or the Highway managers are excessively entrenched in a particular point of view. Having a strong point of view is important, but these leaders risk being so entrenched in their ideas or approaches that they become obstacles to change or effective action by the team. Managers who are excessively entrenched will sometimes listen to others' ideas or recommendations but not act on them. They may use their own experience to legitimize their position but not be open to others' experiences, especially if those experiences contradict what the manager already believes. In extreme cases, they are domineering and may resort to personal attacks if they feel they are "losing."

If you find that your ideas go unchallenged or that your perspective almost always prevails in discussions, then you are probably a My Way or the Highway type. No one is right that much of the time. You may have an excessively high need for power and control and be inflexible. You need to delegate more decisions (and not just the trivial ones) and refuse to interfere when the decision has been made (except in rare cases). You have to delegate more and intervene less. And you need to listen. Start by asking employees for their ideas or perspectives and then adopting the best of them. Finally, find ways to give away the credit. Recognize people for their contributions and force yourself off the center stage.

The Mr. Data

Mr. Data was the humanlike robot in the television series *Star Trek: The Next Generation* who was intellectually brilliant but lacked emotions. Mr. Data managers are too logical, ignoring emotional or people concerns and making decisions based primarily on logic, regardless of the potential negative impacts on people. They are often hardworking and tend to be perfectionists. However, they generally don't believe in small talk and may not be natural relationship builders. They often come up with the "right" answer but cannot get others to buy into it.

You probably know if you're too logical: you're uncomfortable with people problems, you don't like conflict, you hate making decisions unless you have all the facts, you like to dive deep and have all the details, and the part of the job you like most is the analysis. Unfortunately, a lot of what happens in organizations is illogical. Marvin Bower, who helped found the management consulting firm McKinsey and Company, once commented that business people make decisions emotionally and then justify their decisions with logic. Rational decision making obviously has its place, but beware of taking too narrow a view. Of all the ways to influence people, logical persuasion is less effective than any other method. People are far more likely to be persuaded if you involve them in the decision, appeal to their values, socialize with them and find commonalities, and if you appeal to their collegiality or friendship.

The It's My Baby

It's My Baby managers are too possessive of their work products. They generally work long hours, sometimes to the detriment of their private lives. They tend to hire people or team with people who are believers or followers, and their sense of ownership for their work may interfere with their judgment. So, while pride of ownership is good, it's important to maintain a balance between possessing the idea or project and sharing the feelings of ownership with others.

You will know if you are an It's My Baby type if you typically work long hours, give up evenings and weekends, and feel as though no one else is experienced enough, knowledgeable enough, or capable enough to get the results and achieve the level of quality you expect. You also fall into this archetype if you insist on having your hand in everything. When I coach managers like this, I ask them to imagine what would happen if they were hit by a bus. Who would take over? Who would assume responsibility? How would the projects continue and be completed? How would people rise to the occasion? This dialogue usually helps them see that they have better people working for them than they thought and that the best of these people would carry on despite their absence. None of us is as indispensable as we'd like to believe, and when you recognize that and help your employees develop their skills and assume more responsibility, they and the company grow.

The Ostrich

The Ostriches are excessively detailed. Although paying attention to details is usually a virtue, these leaders focus too much on the details of a project and become micromanagers and doers rather than leaders and strategists. At the extreme, managers who obsess over details can be controlling and domineering, especially under pressure. They often control key information and are reluctant to put other people into stretch roles.

If you are an Ostrich leader, you are likely to be a perfectionist and nitpicky. You may want to read project or report summaries but will also scrutinize the details. You may find yourself working at home late at night to catch up on the things you couldn't get done during the workday. The key to overcoming this pattern is trust. At some point, you have to trust that others have taken care of the details and that the high-level summary they give you is sufficient. To reach this point, however, you must trust your people to do the job, and you must decide that you don't have to have command of all the details. I suspect that many Ostrich types bury themselves in the details because secretly they love to know everything. It may not be about power and control as much as it is about the sheer joy of knowing. If that's the case for you, then you still need to decide when to deep dive and when to stay shallow because you probably can't dive deep on everything without damaging your health, your sanity, your family life, and, ultimately, your organization.

The Lone Wolf Leader Types

The four Lone Wolf leader types are characterized by excessive dominance, control, or autonomy. Although they operate from within organizations and systems, they prefer to work by themselves or to put others in strictly subordinate roles.

The General MacArthur

Like the World War II and Korean War general, the General MacArthur types are excessively independent. Although independent thought and initiative are important, these managers often don't want to be accountable to anyone and may discount their reliance on other people.

Leaders who are excessively independent usually have inflated self-concepts and a very high need for power and control. They often will not cooperate with their peers and may hoard information as a way to exercise control. In some cases, business unit heads have so much autonomy that they rule their own private fiefdoms and refuse to act for the greater good or be responsive to a new CEO. It's a very unhealthy situation and is often resolved only when the CEO (usually with the board's endorsement) removes the most independent of the business unit managers, asserts his or her legitimate authority, and compels the remaining business unit heads to cooperate with one another.

The Mule

The Mule leaders are excessively stubborn. Although it is good to have a strong perspective, these types of managers must be careful about appearing intransigent and unwilling to compromise. People who are excessively stubborn are often not open to divergent opinions, are resistant to change, and may argue that "we've always done things this way."

If you observe that you've been digging in your heels or reacting defensively when someone challenges your perspective, then you are in danger of mulelike behavior. The obvious problem is that this kind of behavior breeds on itself. The manager behaves stubbornly as a rote response to any challenge and thus discourages people from speaking up when they should. There is no quick fix for excessive stubbornness. You just have to recognize when it's become a pattern for you and try to be more reasonable when challenged or questioned. Mules are typically bad listeners, so if you are receiving that feedback, then you may be falling into this dark-side type.

The Might Is Right

The Might Is Right managers are domineering. They hold strong views and usually play legitimately strong roles in their areas. They have to beware, however, of using power and intimidation as their primary forms of influence. At the most extreme, managers who are domineering are hierarchical, justify their behavior through position or force, are sometimes caustic or abrasive, and make public examples of those who dissent. None of these behaviors will sustain relationships or build goodwill.

If you feel strongly about your ideas, have an outgoing or forceful personality, and are articulate, you can be perceived as a Might Is Right type of manager simply because you are so persuasive. One of the executives I coached was a tall, handsome man with a powerful presence who people thought was arrogant and domineering simply because he carried himself well and had a charismatic personality. I had to coach him how to use his gifts selectively. However, dominant behavior can occur if a manager lacks those natural gifts and is trying to compensate by behaving more forcefully. To overcome this type, avoid being the loudest person in the room, avoid trying to win arguments through volume or persistence, and avoid being too forceful physically. Each of these strategies is alienating and damages or destroys relationships.

The Power Player

The Power Player types are controlling, particularly around information. They view information as power and guard it zealously. They also solve problems by themselves and then tell others what the solution is rather than involve them. They may want to verify their solutions with others but usually neither get nor truly value input from others. They stay mostly on their own agendas, so they do not listen as well as they should, and they frequently believe that their hierarchical positions justify their behavior.

Power Player leaders can be infuriating to work with. When someone points out that this type of manager has neglected to share an important piece of information, the Power Player might feign innocence and say, "Oh, I thought you already knew that" or "I assumed you were copied on that." The Power Player is about control but doesn't want to appear to be uncooperative. This leader type is insecure and fearful and tries to mask it by hoarding information and using it selectively to achieve his or her goals.

The Deceiver Leader Types

These types of leaders lack integrity and act out of self-interest. They try to control the world by manipulating the truth.

The Crook

The Crook types are excessively self-interested and self-promoting. They do whatever is best for themselves, regardless of the cost to employees, shareholders, or the organization. They often push gray areas, follow their own code of conduct, and look for ways to increase their own advantage. In the worst cases, they break the law or otherwise engage in unethical behavior. An example of this is Andrew Fastow, former chief financial officer for Enron. His off-the-book schemes and financial chicanery helped destroy the seventh-largest corporation in the world and wiped out billions in retirement savings for people and institutions who trusted him and his coconspirators.

The Crooks are mainly self-interested people of low integrity. They have little regard for others and are willing to dissemble in order to turn things in their favor. Managers of this type from Adelphia, WorldCom, Tyco, Enron, HealthSouth, and many other corporations have destroyed billions in shareholder value in the past decade in order to line their own pockets. These are shameful examples of abuse of the trust we place in people in management positions.

The Cokehead

The Cokehead type includes managers who are dependent on something—often drugs, alcohol, gambling, or sex. They can appear impulsive, aggressive, erratic, and even antisocial or alienated from others. They may have trouble planning and organizing, may miss meetings or other commitments, may neglect hygiene or nutrition, and otherwise engage in odd or quirky behavior.

If you have dependency disorder, you will probably have close friends or family telling you that you're drinking too much, gambling too much, or engaging in some other activity to excess. Often close friends are the ones who have permission to tell you the truth and will give you the first signs that there's an issue. You will probably react by denying it, because you don't want to face up to the problem. You need to admit to yourself that you have a problem and get help for it before you destroy your family, your life, your career, and your organization.

The Shortcut

The Shortcut types are willing to bend the rules to increase their gain. Their incursions into the gray area are small at first but gradually become larger until they are firmly on the dark side, often arriving there before they realize it. These managers follow the path of least resistance and are willing to take small, incremental steps that reflect questionable judgment or practice. They not only bend the rules, they often teach their employees to do the same, until the whole organization is behaving unethically. I often refer to such managers as the "white lie people." "It's just a white lie," they say, as if that's okay. They lack a strong moral compass, but they're afraid of getting caught and having to admit their lack of integrity (and have others know them for who they really are). These people lack integrity but want to avoid conflict.

The Pinocchio

The Pinocchio types embrace ambiguity. Sometimes, the situation is not clear and managers have to be deliberately vague, but in excess ambiguity will appear deceptive, and people may assume that these managers are telling half-truths, having selective memory, intentionally withholding information, or spinning the truth to hide problems or to make themselves or their organizations look better. Unlike the Shortcut types, the Pinocchios often strive to be ethical but fail because they don't want to bear bad tidings. So they shade the truth, try to make things look better than they are, or give information selectively so people don't become alarmed. Clearly, this pattern is problematic and will eventually destroy trust. The primary failing of many Pinocchios is lack of candor.

The Bridge Burner Leader Types

The Bridge Burners have a history of negative relationships. They tend to be too aggressive and have too little regard for other people.

The Duelist

The Duelist types are overly aggressive. Being appropriately assertive is an important skill, but assertiveness carried to an extreme turns into win-lose aggression. The Duelists usually describe themselves as being competitive and see that as a virtue, but their competitiveness is all about winning, typically at someone else's expense. They generally have a high need for power and control, are critical, have little generosity, and are not collaborative. To them, life is a contest, and they'll often do just about anything to win.

If you tend to fall into this pattern of behavior, you will probably say that you enjoy conflict and love a good debate. You may engage in competitive activities such as running, rowing, tennis, or a team sport. You probably hate to lose at anything, and may become depressed or surly if things don't go your way. There's nothing wrong with competition, of course, but if you carry it to an extreme you may wind up paying a heavy price for your wins, including damaged relationships. To avoid that, you need to be able to lose gracefully, place even more emphasis on collaboration, and not make others feel like losers if they are not as competitive as you are. And don't disagree with people just for the sake of disagreeing. It invalidates them and their ideas and accomplishes nothing.

The Passive-Aggressive

Unlike the Duelist, the Passive-Aggressive types are excessively conflict averse. If managers feel aggressive but don't want to express their aggression directly, they can become passive-aggressive, which means publicly agreeing with people but privately undermining them. There is no visible, outward conflict, and when confronted, Passive-Aggressive types will appear to agree but resist passively. This kind of behavior can appear to be negatively political and even manipulative.

Some business cultures are passive-aggressive, where the norm is never to make waves publicly or disagree with someone when the disagreement might create conflict. Instead of disagreeing with a decision or position during a meeting, people appear to agree with the decision but then talk it down in the hallways afterward and fail to implement the decision. The gap between the espoused values and the values in practice is huge. When the norm is to passively resist, everyone becomes political and manipulative. It creates a frustrating place to work because you never really know where anyone stands, and you can't engage in the healthy debates that are required for optimizing ideas and solutions.

You will know if you behave passive-aggressively if you don't like to make waves in public; are reluctant to challenge people, especially people more senior to you; and find that you get most things done by working behind the scenes or making side deals with people one-on-one. To break out of this pattern, you need to speak up and be candid about what you believe, no matter how much debate it might cause. As a manager you need to be candid and direct because you set the tone for how others will behave in your group.

The Sledgehammer

As the name implies, this leader type is excessively harsh. It's all right to disagree with someone or to oppose a plan, but these managers let it become personal. They tend to personalize feedback and may attack people verbally. They seem generally discontented and angry at the world. Sledgehammer types are especially harsh when they are pressured, stressed, or angry.

The Sledgehammers are generally not very self-aware. They usually consider themselves to be tough-minded businesspeople. "Sure, I'm tough on people," they might say. "You have to push people to get anything done." Or they'll call themselves demanding or exacting. They may pride themselves on having "pit bull personalities." They occasionally delude themselves by thinking that they are "tough but fair."

The User

As the name implies, the Users use people, and their partners, colleagues, and employees eventually learn to see what's behind the facade. These leaders operate almost entirely out of self-interest and think of people as pawns. If they are nice to people, it's because they can get what they want by being nice. If they are distant, it's because they think distance will work better than some other approach. Everything they do is calculated and often devious.

Most Users are unaware that they are being false and manipulative. They can fool themselves into thinking that they are just politically savvy or clever about knowing how to "play the game." They are often cynical by nature and believe that this is just how the world works. At heart, they really don't care about others and view people mostly as a means to an end.

The Great Leader Archetype: The Egomaniacs

The Great Leader is a person characterized by excessive self-concept, self-interest, and a high need for power. These egomaniacs are all about themselves.

These proud and vain leaders often put themselves ahead of the company, are overly focused on rewards and self-recognition, tend to be condescending or arrogant, and build their own personal brand to the exclusion of everyone else. At the extreme, they can be manipulative, can become angry if someone seems to be working against them, tend not to trust many people, are poor listeners, and tend to make people dependent on them.

These managers are generally high performers whose egos become dangerously inflated because they in fact do perform well. They get results, are publicly recognized for their accomplishments, and are typically promoted quickly to higher and higher positions because they are gifted and perform well. The problem occurs when their success goes to their heads and they start behaving as though they are more godlike than human. They lose their sense of perspective and start thinking of themselves as extraordinarily gifted or special.

Avoiding the Dark Side

More managers than you might imagine fall into the dark side. We hear mainly of the most publicized cases—Jeffrey Skilling, Kenneth Lay, and Andrew Fastow at Enron; Martha Stewart; Leona Helmsley; David Radler of Ravelston Corporation; Dennis Kozlowski and Mark Swartz at Tyco; John and Timothy Rigas at Adelphia; Bernie Ebbers at WorldCom;

Jill Barad at Mattel; and so on. However, there are legions of lesser-known managers who become excessively logical, entrenched, detailed, manipulative, ambiguous, self-interested, harsh, one-sided, aggressive, conflict averse, or vain. If you lose your balance, it's easy to step into the dark side.

The best way to avoid the dark side is to hold onto your humanity and your humility. Guard them as though they were the treasures they are. Remember that whatever your lot in life, it is transitory. No matter how high you soar, others have soared higher, and you are as human as everyone else on the planet, no matter how successful you become (as you define success). No matter how much power you have or how many people you manage or how much money you make, like everyone else in this world you are one heartbeat away from being a memory.

As simple as it sounds, you avoid the dark side by staying in the light: by living ethically, by being worthy of trust, by respecting others as much as you respect yourself, by being sensitive toward others and managing them as human beings rather than resources, by doing the best you can and not cutting corners, by using power and authority wisely, by listening and keeping an open mind, by being genuine and genuinely interested in what others have to say, by collaborating more than you compete, by recognizing others and sharing the credit, and by keeping an even keel. Below are a few other tips. The other chapters in this book mostly contain "do" lists. This is a "don't" list.

- **Don't be abrasive.** At times, all of us are in bad moods, but abrasiveness becomes a behavioral style when you routinely ignore other people's feelings. Like sandpaper, abrasiveness wears people raw quickly.

- **Don't be the loudest person in the room.** Volume is not power. If you have one of those voices that carries, be sensitive to this and try to lower your voice, particularly when you are discussing sensitive or personal issues where others might overhear you.

- **Don't be overbearing.** Don't try to overwhelm others with your power, authority, physical size, or powers of speech. This is a special concern for large people because they can physically dominate so easily. However, people of any size and shape can be pushy, and pushy people typically don't respect turn taking, which means they have less respect for others' rights and privileges than they do for their own.

- **Don't bully people intellectually.** Some people who have facile minds develop a need to show off, to demonstrate their quickness and cleverness, thus proving the superiority they imagine themselves to have. They need to win all the arguments, to make everything a contest. For some, it is a means of compensating for broader feelings of inadequacy, usually social.

- **Don't be condescending.** Don't treat people as though they are beneath you.

- **Don't minimize others' contributions.** Some people need to elevate their own sense of importance by minimizing what others contribute. People with a number of personality disorders—notably narcissism—have this characteristic.

- **Don't impose yourself on others.** Don't go where you aren't welcome. If someone isn't inviting you, then beware of inviting yourself. They may have valid reasons for not including you. Respect that and give them the space.

- **Don't attack the person rather than the problem.** Even when someone is at fault, it almost never helps to blame the person rather than the problem. If you blame the person, you make them the object of your criticism and almost invariably cause them to become defensive. When you attack the problem, you take the focus away from them and enable them to save face, even when they are at fault.

■ **Don't be manipulative.** Don't withhold information that others need in order to force them to do something that's not in their best interest. In particular, don't disguise your real intentions. People who deceive others about their real intentions can often do so with consummate skill. Sociopaths and con artists use manipulation virtually as an art form.

■ **Don't use flattery as a tool.** Don't offer insincere praise as a way to get others to do things for you. Flattery is disingenuous and as such is the antithesis of graceful living.

■ **Don't use threats.** Don't directly or indirectly use threats as a way to enforce your will on others. Threats are the most egregious way to take away another person's freedom of choice.

■ **Don't be drawn into pointless conflicts.** When conflicts occur, the key question to ask yourself is, which is more important to you—the ideas or the relationship? If the relationship is more important, then accommodate or collaborate.

■ **Don't try to reason with someone who is in the throes of anger.** When the other person is being angry and irrational, don't try to find a reasonable outcome. People can't reason while they're mad. Instead of being suckered into an argument no one can win, just listen, try to understand the person's perspective, and let him or her cool off. Then talk.

■ **Always look at the big picture.** We may be inclined to respond to each circumstance, each moment of frustration, or each person's immediate shortcoming. But the big picture, the context in which things occur, is often a mitigating factor and enables us to see why things happened the way they did or the greater contributions a person makes. It's important to make decisions, especially human decisions, by looking at the general rather than the particular.

■ **Don't try to "win" at interpersonal relationships.** Relationships are not contests.

One of the most important lessons I've learned in managing and relating to others is to try to be more of an adult than the other person. One of the managers I coached some years ago had been in one of those pointless feuds with another manager, one of his colleagues, for quite some time. Neither would back down or apologize—or collaborate with the other. Their feud wasn't hurting the business directly, but it wasn't helping either. I told the executive I was advising that sometimes you need to suck it up and ignore the insults, the frustrations, and the pointless abrasions. Do the right thing, even if you have to be the first to accommodate and apologize, and even if the other person doesn't reciprocate or meet you halfway. Be more of an adult than he or she is.

My client followed this advice—and it worked. Within a short period, the wounds were healed enough for the two to begin working more closely. They probably won't ever like each other, but you never know. Stranger things have happened. When you are more adult than the other person, you set the stage for putting aside the interpersonal issues, petty conflicts, jealousies, and irrational behavior that get in the way of productive relationships—and you avoid behaving badly yourself.

There is a wonderful moment in a little-known and highly underrated film called K2, which fictionalizes the real-life experiences of Seattle lawyer Jim Wickwire and his climbing partner, biophysicist Lou Reichardt, who are considered to be the first Americans to reach the summit of the world's second-highest mountain, K2, which they accomplished on September 6, 1978. In this film, the leading characters Taylor (played by Michael Biehn) and Harold (played by Matt Craven) are alone in their tent at the base camp prior to the summit attempt. Taylor has been behaving arrogantly and self-centeredly and Harold talks to him about his bad behavior. Taylor responds, "I didn't make the world the way it is, Harold. I'm just trying to get through it as fast and clean as possible."

Harold replies, "We all make the world the way it is."

Taylor is an honorable character in his own way, but he is insensitive and narcissistic. Without the moral grounding that Harold provides, Taylor would be hopelessly egotistical and would make a terrible manager. So Harold's lesson is critical: We all make the world the way it is. You can't excuse your behavior by saying that other people do it, or it's just the way things are, or you've earned the right, or whatever other excuse you might offer. You make your own world the way it is. As the manager of others, you create the way things are, the way things work.

Managers are not victims of circumstances. They can and should make choices. They can choose to be stand-up managers, inspiring leaders, great human beings. Or they can choose to be the opposite. The difference between the two extremes is attitude, intention, and character.

Tips for Improving Your Relationships

1. Don't be abrasive.

2. Don't be the loudest person in the room.

3. Don't be overbearing.

4. Don't bully people intellectually.

5. Don't be condescending.

6. Don't minimize others' contributions.

7. Don't impose yourself on others.

8. Don't attack the person rather than the problem.

9. Don't be manipulative.

10. Don't use flattery as a tool.

11. Don't use threats.

12. Don't be drawn into pointless conflicts.

13. Don't try to reason with someone who is in the throes of anger.

14. Always look at the big picture.

15. Don't try to "win" at interpersonal relationships.

Afterword

I've met managers who loved their jobs but hated managing people, which may seem contradictory at first but isn't. What they loved was being in charge, solving problems, making decisions, having the authority and responsibility to achieve results, and so on; what they disliked was having to resolve conflicts, deal with substandard performance issues, respond to complaints, motivate people whom they thought should have been self-motivating, fix dysfunctional teams, react to employees who were demanding more compensation for no more work, and fire people who were unproductive or disruptive.

Without question, management can be frustrating, exhausting, and disheartening, but it can also be exhilarating, energizing, and fun. Whether it's fun or not depends on how you view the journey. If you truly despise handling people problems, perhaps you should consider a change to a role where you can be a brilliant individual contributor or run a smaller operation with fewer people. Ultimately, if you don't enjoy what you're doing, you will never be able to bring to it the energy and joy necessary to make it satisfying for everyone else. Besides, life is too short to devote years to an activity that drains and dissatisfies you.

Very few people enjoy dealing with tough people issues at work, and if you have a lot of them to deal with, there may be a broader problem with your company or the environment you are working in. However, most managers work in situations where the people challenges, as tough as they might be, are normal. The fact is that no business runs smoothly all the time, even the best employees occasionally go off track, and there will be conflicts, problems, and other bumps in the road as part of the normal course of events. You can't avoid that.

The managers I've met who coped best with the vagaries of management in organizations were those who expected problems, took them in stride, kept an even keel, and found ways to enjoy the journey no matter how rough the waves became. Here are some ways to do that.

Keep Your Perspective

Perhaps the most important thing to do when you are burdened with pressures and challenges is to keep things in perspective. Every time you need to react to a situation or make a decision, especially a tough one where there are no clear answers, pause for a moment and think about the context. What's going on? How important is this? What would happen if you don't make the decision now? What are the implications of waiting, of doing nothing, or of acting sooner? What's the other side of the equation?

It's easy to become immersed in the downside of issues and let the stress build to the point that you feel nothing but the strain and the gloom. To avoid that, step back now and then and reflect on the context in which the situation is occurring and how important things are. Some years ago I was playing racquetball with a colleague, and as he leaped for the ball, he swung wildly and hit me with his racket. Later, as a doctor was sewing up the sizable wound on my forehead, I told him I was worried about scarring, and he said, "Look at it this way. In a hundred years, no one will care." I've recalled his comment many times as I dealt with management crises, and it's helped me keep things in perspective.

Find a Collaborative Partner

The management life is sometimes stressful and lonely. One of the ways to make it more fun is to have a confidante or collaborative partner with whom you can talk about the challenges, frustrations, and triumphs. A boss can play that role, but more often it's a mentor, colleague, friend, spouse, or significant other. You need someone in your life who can listen, empathize, play devil's advocate, challenge, advise you, and otherwise be there when you need some breathing space.

One of the most difficult aspects of being a manager is that the position isolates you, often from the people who used to be friends. At the higher levels in organizations, collegial relationships are sometimes strained because the people in senior roles feel as if they are competing for the relatively few positions at the very top of the organization. When people compete with one another, they typically don't confide in one another or reveal their anxieties or frustrations. But you need an outlet, someone who will listen well, act with your best interests in mind, offer objective guidance, and be helpful without having a hidden agenda.

Know What You Thrive On

According to Maryann Billington, one of my colleagues at Lore, to make the management journey enjoyable you have to know what you thrive on and find ways to intersperse that with the difficult and more challenging parts of the job. For Maryann, it's making people successful. She thrives on seeing others do well, so she tries to balance the opportunity to see others do well with the parts of the job that are not as much fun for her. It's about balance. What you have to do, she says, is manage the ups with the downs. If you can do enough of what you thrive on, then you'll even out the rough spots and make the tougher parts of management more tolerable.

Take Time-Outs

For me, it's essential now and then to take a time-out. If I can, I'll do a movie matinee with a colleague or family member, take a long walk, go shopping, listen to music, or go home and play with my dogs. Sometimes, for the sake of your mental health, you just need to get away. I do it during the business day rather than on the weekend because I want the time-out to be a deliberate break from work. Whatever your source of relaxation or satisfaction, the key is to get away momentarily and do something completely different and maybe completely for yourself.

Find the Opportunity at the Heart of Every Problem

Yes, I know this advice is not new, but like many clichés this one carries not only a gem of truth but a virtual gold mine. The finest managers I've worked with are optimistic and resilient. No matter what problems they face, they invariably find ways to turn adversity into opportunity. More than just a part of their character, the optimism and resilience they show is a fundamental attitude about life—that it's worth living, that problems are a natural part of life, that everything can be overcome (although the outcome may not be exactly as you'd hoped for or expected), and that no matter how things work out, they were undoubtedly meant to work out that way.

Search for the Joy in Leading Others

If you are not naturally a people person, this one may seem hard, but there is joy in seeing others thrive. It's satisfying to build something and see others not only take it over and run with it but transform it into something greater and grander than you might have imagined. It's satisfying to coach or mentor someone and see that person's performance, attitude, and prospects improve. It's satisfying to see a team that you've created hit its stride and start producing at record levels. If you don't find pleasure in these things, then you aren't really a leader and should go do something else. However, if you can grow people and then stand back and watch them thrive, then you have one of the fundamental attributes of an outstanding leader/manager.

Accept That Sometimes Your Best People Will Leave

An often difficult part of managing an organization is seeing your best people leave. Whether they are retiring, transferring to another division in your company, or leaving to take a job with someone else, it's difficult to watch these people leave, particularly if you've been instrumental in helping them grow and develop their skills. One of the ironies of outstanding management and leadership is that, by your excellence, you create your own problems. By leading, challenging, growing, and coaching your people, particularly your most talented people, you turn them into the highly qualified, experienced, and capable people who will seek better opportunities if your organization can't continue to find more challenging and rewarding roles for them.

It's how the world works. People come to you, learn a great deal from you, contribute to your success while you contribute to theirs, and then they leave you to find better opportunities than your company can offer them. This is a natural part of organizational life, and it's best to let them go on as positive a basis as possible. Then maybe they will remain friends and will return the favor later.

Accept That Not Everyone Is a Good Fit

You also have to accept that not everyone who works for you will be a good fit, and you may need to let them go. I hired a secretary many years ago who wound up reading romance novels at her desk during the workday. I told her point-blank that this behavior was unacceptable, but she kept doing it when she thought no one would notice. I would have let her go much earlier than I did, but I felt sorry for her because she was a single mother with a two-year-old daughter. It took me a while to learn that you do no favors for people if you keep them on when they are clearly not a good fit. It's best to cut your losses early and do what is ultimately more humane for them and better for your company.

I've learned to tell people that the organization is what it is. We do what we do. If you like that and can find passion in doing the job, then this place is a good fit for you. Work should be fun—good, professional fun. The people who engage in it should like what they're doing. If they don't, they should go elsewhere to find their bliss.

Celebrate from Time to Time

Finally, the way to enjoy the journey is to celebrate from time to time. Celebrate your successes and milestones. Celebrate the big wins (and some of the small ones). Celebrate new hires and promotions. Celebrate your clients or customers. Celebrate the end of the week. Celebrate for no reason at all except that you're alive, you're breathing, you're working, you're contributing to the world, and you're doing something meaningful with your life.

Enjoy the journey.

Tips for Improving Your Relationships

1. Keep your perspective.

2. Find a collaborative partner.

3. Know what you thrive on.

4. Take time-outs.

5. Find the opportunity at the heart of every problem.

6. Search for the joy in leading others.

7. Accept that sometimes your best people will leave.

8. Accept that not everyone is a good fit.

9. Celebrate from time to time.

Appendix

The Research on What People Want from Relationships

Although there have been numerous studies of what motivates people at work, none have focused on what people want from their relationship with their manager or supervisor. To study those relationships, I conducted two research studies through the Lore Research Institute in 2004 and 2005.

Findings from the First Study

In the first, I asked 138 respondents to list what they wanted or expected in their relationships with family and friends and in their nonfamily relationships. I examined the narrative responses, which were mostly words or phrases, and noted the frequency of occurrence of each relationship need. In the order of frequency, here were the top seven groupings for each type of relationship:

Nonfamily Relationships

1. Honesty and integrity
2. Respect, sincerity, positive attitude, and space
3. Clear communication, openness, and listening
4. Support and encouragement, appreciation, and recognition
5. Caring, acceptance, kindness, generosity, consideration and fairness; inclusion and loyalty
6. Collaboration, cooperation, teamwork, and camaraderie
7. Trust

Family and Friend Relationships

1. Love, affection, passion, hugging
2. Trust, keeping confidences
3. Communication, open dialogue, listening, and open-mindedness
4. Honesty and integrity
5. Genuine support, emotional support
6. Understanding, sensitivity, empathy, and compassion
7. Unconditional acceptance, forgiveness, patience, inclusion, faith, and no pressure

This study did not distinguish between people's relationships with their managers and their colleagues or peers. However, it did confirm my assumption that what people want from their families and friends is considerably different from what they want from the people they work with, and it helped me identify fifty-one relationship needs people consider important.

Findings from the Second Study

I used these relationship needs as the basis for a more comprehensive follow-on study in which I asked nearly five hundred respondents to identify how important each of these needs is on a scale of 1 (not important) to 5 (very important).[1] In this study I asked respondents to rate their relationship needs with respect to three types of relationships: (1) managers, (2) colleagues or peers, and (3) close friends or family. Finally, I asked respondents to rate how important these seventeen needs were to them.

- Feeling involved in activities that matter to me
- Being appreciated for who I am and what I do
- Feeling excited about what I'm doing or what's going on
- Being challenged; feeling like I am growing
- Being accepted as myself
- Feeling welcomed by others and encouraged to belong
- Feeling that others care about me
- Feeling that I am informed about what's going on
- Feeling competent and skilled
- Feeling that others trust me
- Feeling that I belong, that I am part of something important, something I care about
- Feeling that others understand me
- Being independent, feeling that I answer to no one
- Feeling that I can be honest with others and they will be honest with me

▧ Feeling good about myself

▧ Feeling that others like me

▧ Feeling that others look up to me and will follow me

The results of this ranking are shown and discussed in Chapter 1. The survey questionnaire included a number of demographic questions: gender, age, introvert or extrovert, manager or not, religious or spiritual or not. I hypothesized that some of these demographic distinctions would yield significant differences in what people wanted from their relationships, and this turned out to be true—spectacularly so in some cases.

To make this book a manageable size, I have not included the detailed findings from the relationship needs study. However, a full research report is available from the Lore Research Institute. Interested readers should contact Lore International Institute at (970) 385-4955 or visit the Web site at www.lorenet.com.

Findings about What Specific Groups of People Want

The following ten tables reveal the findings for five demographic groups of people.

What Men and Women Want

In his popular books on gender differences, author John Gray argues that the ways men and women think, take in information, and communicate are very different.[2] It will come as no surprise, then, that what men and women want from relationships is also quite different—at least in some respects. However, the research on people's relationship needs also shows that there are striking similarities in what men and women want. First, let's look at the similarities.

What Both Men and Women Want
from Manager Relationships

High need for **honesty** and **integrity**	What both men and women want *most* is to know that they can trust their manager to tell the truth, to be forthright and candid. They also want to feel that their manager trusts them. Trust is the bedrock, the fundamental, can't-do-without-it quality in any manager-employee relationship. That's why being worthy of trust is critically important for managers.
High need for **fairness**	Both men and women want to know that their managers will apply the same standards to everyone, treating people equitably and impartially, judging people fairly and without bias.
High need for **discretion**	They also want to know that their managers will be discreet, that they will safeguard sensitive and personal information. Clearly, what people want is a very high standard of integrity.
High need for **respect**	Both men and women have a high need to feel that their managers respect them and hold them in high esteem. All employees need to feel that those in authority regard them positively.
High need for **professionalism**	Finally, both men and women want their managers to behave professionally—to adhere to high standards of conduct, to be knowledgeable and credible, and to be calm in the midst of turmoil, confident in the face of uncertainty, and considerate in their treatment of others.

Everyone wants managers who are honest, respectful, fair, trustworthy, discreet, and professional. So how do women's relationship needs differ from men's? In my respondent group, 57 percent were women and 43 percent were men. Here is what the women said they want.

What Women Want (Compared to Men)	
Greater need for **courtesy** and **consideration**	Women have a far greater need than men for courtesy and consideration from their managers and coworkers. In general, men care less about politeness, maybe because they are less accustomed to it from one another, and women have a greater need for courtesy because of the rules most of us learned in childhood (depending on our upbringing) about how gentlemen are supposed to treat ladies. We could argue that gender roles are changing and women in general may not expect men to be as chivalric as they once were. Nonetheless, the research shows that women have a significantly greater need for courtesy and consideration in their relationships with managers than men do.
Greater need for **feeling valued** and **respected**	Women also have a significantly greater need to feel that their managers value and respect them. On the whole, women need to know that their managers believe they have worth, that they are contributing in meaningful and valuable ways, and that their work is held in high esteem. I would find this need surprising if I hadn't coached hundreds of women, mostly young-to-middle-aged professionals, who had low self-confidence and sometimes questioned whether they were fit for the job they were doing—although they were performing exceptionally well. Some women in business, perhaps a

Greater need for
feeling valued
and **respected**
(cont.)

good many, don't develop the same intrinsic sense of self-worth that their male counterparts do.

As they are growing up, boys learn to project more self-confidence than they often feel. They also learn the difference between assertiveness and aggression. When they are playing with other boys and become too rough, their buddies let them know what the boundaries are and what's acceptable and what isn't. Girls often don't learn this lesson. Their form of play is usually more consensus based and cooperative, so while they learn subtler forms of influence and interaction, they don't necessarily learn how to develop an assertive presence that is socially acceptable. Of course, such generalizations may not hold true for individual boys and girls, but the developmental patterns are, by and large, true.

The result is that when men enter the workplace, many of them possess a degree of confidence that exceeds their abilities, and they have significantly less need than women do to feel valued by their peers or managers. Again, these are broad generalizations. Some men have low self-confidence and some women are supremely self-confident. The bottom-line lesson for managers is that you can bolster *anyone's* self-confidence by showing that you value them and what they contribute—and on the whole women are more likely than men to need this feedback.

Greater need for **rewards** and **recognition**	Women have a significantly greater need for rewards and recognition for their accomplishments from their managers. In other words, they need to see the tangible evidence that they are valued and respected, that their contributions matter, and that they are highly regarded. Men are less likely to need the public recognition and validation, but for most women the recognition among their peer group is extremely important. So managers should ensure, especially for women, that the rewards and recognition are commensurate with the accomplishments and that the recognition occurs publicly or at least among a woman's coworkers and friends. The caveat here, as with any generalization, is that it applies to the group but not necessarily to individuals. You have to know each person and adapt to his or her wishes accordingly.
Greater need for **respect for their space**	Not surprisingly, women also have a significantly greater need for other people to respect their space, and this applies to friends and family as well as managers and coworkers. Why is this true? Perhaps it's because women are inherently more private than men, or perhaps they have a greater need to keep their professional and personal lives separate. Perhaps it's because in the normal mating ritual women are more often the pursued than the pursuers, so they develop a stronger need for personal and psychological boundaries. Maybe it's because women, more often than men, are victims of sexual and other forms of harassment. Whether or not a particular woman has been harassed in the workplace, she knows it happens and could happen to her, so she needs a safer "space" around her than her male colleagues need. Whatever the reasons, women are more likely to want their boundaries respected and maintained.

Greater need to
be listened to

Women are also more likely than men to feel that they aren't being listened to, a finding that probably won't surprise most women. Women's voices are more complex than men's voices and are processed in a different part of the brain than men's voices are. So the reason male managers, in particular, do not listen as well to female employees as they do to fellow males may be neurological in origin. But it may also be because women's voices, which are generally softer and higher in pitch, do not command as much authority as the average male voice, which is deeper, louder, and more resonant. Or maybe it's because some men place less value on what women have to say. I've heard this argument from time to time, and the research supports that women find it more difficult to get air time in team meetings and have more trouble getting their ideas accepted, even when those ideas later prove to be the best ones.

The lesson for managers is that women, as a group, have a greater need to feel listened to. You can meet this need—and here's a breakthrough thought—by actually listening to them, which means focusing on what's being said, reflecting and reinforcing the speaker's thoughts, asking questions based on what you're hearing, synthesizing the speaker's ideas from time to time, and being fully present while she is talking to you. This is certainly not rocket science, but it does require more attentiveness than many managers apply, and it's especially difficult when you're frazzled, burned out, and too busy, which is a normal state for many managers.

Greater need for **cooperation** and **collaboration** and **strong work ethic**

Lastly, women have a greater need than men do for cooperation and collaboration with their coworkers, and they have a significantly greater need than men to feel that their coworkers and managers have a strong work ethic. As a group, women tend to be more collaborative than men, so the need for greater cooperation (and less competition) makes sense. Men are more used to competing with one another and may find individual efforts more satisfying than team efforts, despite the experiences most boys have in team sport activities.

Regarding women's greater need for a strong work ethic in their managers and coworkers, I would speculate that because women are newer to the workplace, they have a stronger need to believe that performance alone is how people should get ahead. Or perhaps a strong work ethic is important in breaking through barriers and breaking down the women-belong-in-the-home stereotypes that existed in the old workplace. Women do feel an acute sense of competition at work, not only with men (who are still on average paid more than women for the same work), but also with other women.

It would be gratifying to know that people advance based on their work ethic and performance rather than by idiosyncratic "rules" among the "old guard." Advancing because you have a strong work ethic is a concept more easily understood and achieved (if you work hard) than advancing because of vague and perhaps discriminatory "old boys' network" rules. It's interesting to speculate why women have a greater need for a strong work ethic in their managers and coworkers, but there probably is no single reason. The professional women I've spoken to about it give varying answers, but most agree that it is very important to them.

What Men Want (Compared to Women)

Greater need for **friendship, companionship,** and **shared interests**

Men have a significantly greater need than women do for friendship, companionship, and shared interests in their relationships with managers and, to a lesser extent, with coworkers. These research results strongly support the notion that men find their friendships at work and that men seek collegial familiarity with those who manage them, particularly other men. The results also suggest what may drive the "old boys' networks" that exist in the workplace as well as in other parts of society. By and large, men want buddies. They form friendships based on shared interests and want to know that the people they work with, especially those who have authority over them, view them as friends and companions and not just as employees.

But it's more than that. Men derive a lot of satisfaction from having common interests with other people (women as well as other men) and from the bonding that takes place when they do things they like to do with other people who like to do them. We could make the same argument for women—except that women seem to have a significantly lower need for shared interests, friendship, and companionship in their relationships *at work,* perhaps because they are more likely to have those needs fulfilled in other areas of their lives. Moreover, because the workplace has traditionally been dominated by men, and because men's interests are more likely to be aligned with other men's interests, men have developed a stronger need for the kind of male bonds at work that they may have experienced with other men on sports teams or in the military. The latter, in particular, is a place where many men form strong male bonds—ones that often last a lifetime.

Greater need for **unconditional acceptance** and **availability**	Men have a greater need for unconditional acceptance from their managers and coworkers (which is what they typically get from their buddies), and they want to know that their managers will be available when they need them, which, again, is what one expects from friends.
	Does this mean that if you are a manager you should seek friendships with your male employees? Not necessarily. In fact, it may be wise to resist forming those kinds of bonds because they can complicate the manager-employee relationship and make it difficult to be unbiased and tough when you need to be, but you should be aware that men as a group are more likely to want a relationship with you that has some elements of friendship and companionship to it. Furthermore, the more you can find shared interests with the men you manage, the more comfortable they are likely to be with you—and the more they are likely to trust you.

What the Young and Old Want

Age mattered in the survey responses, particularly in light of the differences between the baby boomer generation, who are now in their forties through early sixties, and the Generation X group, many of whom are in their thirties and now have children of their own. But the greatest generational differences were between the baby boomers, many of whom are today's managers, and the Generation Y group, who are those born in the 1980s and early 1990s and who are often children of the baby boomers. In the research, people in their twenties made up 8 percent of the respondents; people in their fifties or sixties, 43 percent of the population.

What People in Their Twenties Want
(Compared with Other Age Groups)

Lower need for **shared values**	Compared to people in their forties and fifties, they have a significantly lower need for shared values in all relationships, but particularly from close friends and family. People in their twenties may be more independent because they are the first generation to be raised in an era of widespread personal technology use, including computers, the Internet, and cell phones. Their ready access to technology may encourage strong value independence.
Greater need for **respect for their space**	Their greater need for managers and coworkers or peers to respect their space is another indicator of their strong desire for independence.
Greater need for **unconditional acceptance**	They seem to be saying, "Accept me for who I am, and don't try to change me." They also have a lower need for affection in relationships with close friends and family. Both of these findings are further evidence of this generation's need for independence.
Greater need for **rewards, recognition,** and **appreciation**	They may just be making their way and need positive reinforcement. However, they also seem to have a strong desire for the immediate and concrete. They are not content with vague promises of things to come. Not big on delayed gratification, they have a significantly greater need for appreciation and tangible rewards as soon as they can get them.

Greater need for **mentoring** or **coaching**	They have a greater need than any other age group for mentoring or coaching from their managers. They seem hungry to learn and are eager for help and guidance from their managers.
Greater need for **responsiveness**	They have a greater need for responsiveness from managers than older people do, perhaps because they have an inherently greater need for responsiveness in general, or because as we age we learn to live with less responsiveness from people around us. Or maybe this group, which grew up with laptops and other sophisticated personal technology, expects greater responsiveness because they are used to getting their way by pushing a button or moving a mouse.

These results suggest that to effectively manager younger workers, you have to understand and respect their need for independence and grant them a fair degree of unconditional acceptance while recognizing and rewarding them in the short term for their accomplishments, being as responsive to them as you can, and giving them coaching and mentoring to help them build their skills and self-confidence. What about older workers? How are they different? In my respondent group, these people comprised 43 percent of the population. Following are their results.

What People in Their Fifties and Sixties Want (Compared with Other Age Groups)

Greater need for **affection**	Once we have children and our children have children, we may have a greater need to give and receive affection.
Lower need for **independence**	As we grow older, we may discover how important family is and come to value our interdependence with family and friends in ways younger people have not yet come to appreciate.
Lower need for **coaching,** **mentoring,** and **helpfulness**	It's not that some in this age group aren't continuing to learn and grow, but when you're in your sixties, there are fewer available, credible mentors, and many people at that age feel that they are near the peak of their skills for the jobs they do. When they seek mentoring or coaching, it is largely for new skill or knowledge areas they want to explore.
Lower need for **trust** and **respect**	People in their sixties have a significantly lower need to trust their managers and coworkers or peers. In contrast, people in their fifties have the greatest need for trust, perhaps reflecting the fact that people in their fifties are in the early stages of preparing for retirement and need to trust that the people they work with will not jeopardize their career at that crucial preretirement point.

What Introverts and Extroverts Want from Relationships

Introverts get their energy internally, are more prone to solitary activities, and tend to be drained by prolonged social interactions. Extroverts get their energy externally, are more prone to social activities, and are energized by prolonged interactions with others.

Therefore, in my research it seemed natural to assume that introverts and extroverts would have different needs from their relationships with others. I asked respondents to identify whether they are more introverted or extroverted, and although their self-reported classifications cannot be verified, it is reasonable to assume that most people can make that identification. Of respondents, 38 percent said they are introverted, and 62 percent said extroverted. Results showed that introverts had no significantly greater needs than extroverts, but extroverts had significantly greater needs in an extraordinary number of areas, as shown here.

What Extroverts Want (Compared with Introverts)	
Greater need for **shared interests** and **values**	As one would expect, extroverts had a greater need than introverts to associate with people who think like they do.
Greater need for **loyalty, commitment, dependability** and **reliability,** and **teamwork**	As we would expect, they have a greater need for teamwork. But, contrary to expectations, they also have a greater need for dependability and commitment. Because introverts typically have fewer, deeper relationships, one would expect them to have a greater need for loyalty and commitment, but this is not true.

Greater need for **empathy, forgiveness,** and **compassion**	They have a significantly greater need for empathy and compassion than do introverts, although it's not clear why this is the case.
Greater need for **professionalism** and **strong work ethic**	They want to know that their workplace interactions are professional, perhaps because they seek more interactions with people, or perhaps because their greater sociability makes it more important that their words and actions are not misinterpreted by the people they work with.
Greater need for **encouragement, mentoring** or **coaching, advice, constructive feedback,** and **helpfulness**	Not surprisingly, they want help and guidance from the people they work with, especially their coworkers. They are more likely than introverts to seek advice and coaching and want the people they work with to give them constructive feedback and encouragement.
Greater need to **feel valued** and **feel understood**	They need to feel that their coworkers value and understand them. Introverts, being more private and internally focused, seem to derive more of their sense of self-worth from their own self-valuation.
Greater need for **cheerfulness, happiness,** and **a good sense of humor**	The stereotype of extroverts is that they are more vivacious, outgoing, friendly, and so on, and this appears to be true. They are more likely than introverts to value cheerful, fun-loving people like themselves.
Greater need for **intellectual stimulation** and **interesting conversation**	They desire intellectual stimulation and interesting conversation more than introverts do. Introverts also need stimulation and want interesting conversations, but they may well be satisfied by talking to fewer people. However, the qualifier may be "with how many people?" Extroverts probably want more conversations with more people.

What People Persons Want from Relationships

In my research on what people want from relationships, I asked respondents to identify whether or not they considered themselves "a people person." I did not define the term beyond that because I think everyone has an intuitive sense of what it means, and I think they know whether or not they enjoy people, enjoy being with people, and have an affinity for people. With the caveat that respondents self-selected whether or not they consider themselves "people persons," a statistical analysis of the results shows some significant differences between those who did self-identify as people persons and those who did not. Of those in the research study, 61 percent considered themselves to be people persons.

What People Persons Want
(Compared with Non–People Persons)

Greater need for **trust, respect, emotional support, open-mindedness, encouragement, caring,** and **consideration**

In their relationships with their managers, people persons have a significantly greater need for trust, respect, emotional support, open-mindedness, encouragement, caring, and consideration than those who do not consider themselves people persons. They need to know that their managers understand and value them and are committed to them. Although these findings seem intuitively obvious, it's interesting to see that the research supports them. People persons have a greater need for human connection, for the kind of emotional resonance in relationships that builds stronger, more personal bonds. They will not do as well with cold, distant, highly technical managers who create little or no human spark. What animates a people person is the warmth, caring, and support found in closer human connections.

Greater need for **shared interests** and **open, candid communication**	They also have a significantly greater need for shared interests with their managers and for open and candid communication. They want to feel some commonality, some points where they and their manager are interested in the same things, perhaps because they seek connections, and shared interests are a wonderful nexus for conversation.
Greater need for **constructive feedback**	They want honest communication, and they have a greater need than their counterparts for constructive feedback from their managers. They hate hidden agendas and prefer that people say whatever needs to be said. People persons will not thrive in passive-aggressive environments (where conflict is hidden and people say one thing to your face and something else behind your back). They typically despise environments that are highly political and where colleagues face cutthroat competition with each other.
Greater need for **teamwork; collaboration** and **cooperation; advice, coaching,** or **mentoring; fairness; genuineness;** and **strong work ethic**	As we would expect, people persons have a significantly greater need for teamwork and collaboration and cooperation. Naturally enough, they want to work with others, and they prefer environments in which challenges and accomplishments are collective rather than individual. They value managers and coworkers who will offer advice and coaching or mentoring when asked for it, and they want to work with people who are fair and genuine and have a strong work ethic.
Greater need for **feeling excited about what they are doing**	They have a significantly greater need to feel excited about what they are doing or what's going on. They want to feel emotionally charged by the work they do. If it becomes dull, they hate it. They need to feel good about themselves and feel that others like them. They need to have both an intrinsic sense of self-worth and extrinsic validation of themselves.

What Non–People Persons Want
(Compared with People Persons)

Lower need for **shared values** and **loyalty**	They have a significantly lower need for shared values with their managers and a significantly lower need for loyalty with their peers. As we might expect, non–people persons tend to work more independently, and they don't want to feel that they rely on others for anything.
Greater need for **friendship**	Curiously, they have a higher need for friendship with their managers, perhaps because they don't have strong bonds elsewhere in the workplace or because they place more value on friendship with the people who have more influence over their work life.
Greater need for **professionalism**	They seem to want both closeness and distance, to have their managers behave professionally but also be friendly.
Greater need for **independence**	Most telling, they have a significantly greater need to be independent, to feel that they answer to no one. It's not simply that they want to work alone or be left alone, they don't want to feel responsible for anyone or feel directed or controlled by anyone. People who describe themselves as non–people persons may truly be lone wolves, which is not criticism but simply a recognition that they work best alone and in situations in which they can be almost entirely self-directed.

What Spiritual or Religious People Want from Relationships

As I researched relationship needs, I wondered whether people who consider themselves spiritual or religious might want something different in relationships from what people who do not consider themselves spiritual or religious want. I did not make a value judgment about either group. I was simply curious about whether feelings of spirituality would matter in what people wanted in their relationships with managers, coworkers, and close friends or family.

I assumed that people who actively practice religion would say that they are spiritual but so would some people without a religious affiliation. On the other hand, some people would not consider themselves religious or spiritual at all. In the interpersonal needs survey, respondents had the option to identify themselves as "religious or spiritual" or "not religious or spiritual." They could also choose a third option: "*somewhat* religious or spiritual." Of the more than 500 people who responded to the survey, 46 percent said they are "religious or spiritual," 38 percent claimed to be "somewhat religious or spiritual," and 16 percent said they are "not religious or spiritual."

What Religious or Spiritual People Want (Compared with Nonreligious or Nonspiritual People)

Greater need for **forgiveness**	Most religions teach forgiveness as a core principle, so it's no surprise that people who consider themselves to be spiritual have a significantly greater need than nonspiritual people for a tolerant and forgiving environment at work and at home. They need relationships in which transgressions are accepted as inevitable and part of being human and in which learning is possible. "Zero defect" and intolerant managers are unlikely to work well with spiritual people.

Greater need for **love** and **emotional support**	Spiritual or religious people have a significantly greater need for love and emotional support in relationships with coworkers or peers. I understood this finding to refer to "brotherly" love, and I think it reflects both religious teachings and the spiritual sense of connectedness with other people. Interestingly, there was no distinction between men or women who consider themselves spiritual—they uniformly had a greater need for emotional support from their managers and "brotherly" love from their coworkers.
Greater need for **courtesy**	Religious people have a significantly greater need for courtesy, I suspect in part because religious groups tend to be traditional and to reinforce social norms, sometimes strictly so. The research did not distinguish between people who consider themselves religious as opposed to spiritual, so it's not clear whether spiritual people would have as great a need for courtesy. Of course, some people who are not religious now were raised in a religious or spiritual environment, so those early influences would be present. Still, it seems likely that the difference lies in the conservative and traditional norms and roles that religions reinforce, where courtesy is practiced and expected.
Greater need to feel **valued** and **accepted unconditionally**	These people have a greater need to feel that their managers value them and accept them unconditionally. Unconditional acceptance is fundamental to most religions, particularly Zen Buddhism, which teaches followers to accept the world as it really is and to accept yourself as you truly are. Most religions also teach that human life is intrinsically valuable and that each of us has merit as a human being. What we learn from such teachings tends to carry over into our working lives, where our learning forms expectations and our expectations become needs.

Greater need to **trust others**	Spiritual people have a greater need to feel that they can trust others. Perhaps they need to have faith in others or believe in the essential goodness in people. In any case, they want to know that they can trust their managers and coworkers. They also have a significantly greater need to feel that they can be honest with others and others can be honest with them.
Greater need for **dependability** and **reliability**	Religious or spiritual people have a significantly greater need for dependability and reliability from their managers.

What emerges from the research is the conclusion that religious or spiritual people have a high need for integrity in the people they work with. They want to be able to trust others and to rely and depend upon them. They also want to feel accepted, emotionally supported, and even loved in a brotherly way.

For the people who were "somewhat religious or spiritual," there were only two areas of significant difference between them and the other two groups: They had a significantly lower need for *affection* in relationships with close friends and family and they had a significantly lower need for *companionship* in their working relationships. There were far more dramatic findings from the 16 percent of people who said they are not religious or spiritual, and in every case what characterized this group was a significantly lower need for many relationship elements, especially compared to those who consider themselves very religious or spiritual.

What Nonreligious or Nonspiritual People Want (Compared with Religious or Spiritual People)

Lower need for **shared values**	This group had a significantly lower need for shared values, especially in their close friends and family relationships. They also had a considerably lower need to feel that their friends and family value them. As a group, they appear to have a degree of value independence from those one would expect to be closest to them. This probably reflects a strong need to find and assert their own value system apart from the values they may have learned from their family as they were raised. Moreover, if they came from a religious or spiritual family, they may feel some rejection or alienation and thus assert that it's less important to them if their friends and family value them.
Lower need for **trust, honesty** and **integrity,** and **strong work ethic**	These people had a significantly lower need to feel trusted by their managers and coworkers. They also had a significantly lower need for honesty and integrity in all their relationships. Honesty and integrity composed the highest-rated need among all other groups, so this group's departure from this norm is noteworthy. I should point out that although this need is significantly lower compared to the "very" or "somewhat" religious groups, it is still among the highest-rated needs for people who do not consider themselves religious or spiritual. Still, this is a highly significant finding. This group also had a significantly lower need for a strong work ethic from their managers, a finding that is difficult to explain. It could be that this group is more realistic about people and less optimistic in its view of human nature. In short, nonreligious people may be more jaded in their views of their managers and not expect as much as people with religious or spiritual beliefs.

Lower need for **loyalty** and **unconditional acceptance**	The nonreligious people had a significantly lower need for coworkers to be loyal to them and to accept them unconditionally. Again, this may reflect a more jaded or "realistic" view of people.
Lower need for **compassion** and **respect**	They had a significantly lower need for compassion from their managers and a lower need for respect from everyone they worked with. Perhaps compassion is less important to them because it is not as central in their moral landscape as it is with people who practice religion or are naturally spiritual. Certainly, most religions teach compassion as a core principle. Respect is also a core need among human beings, and it's not clear why nonreligious or spiritual people have a significantly lower need for it. Does this mean that they don't feel they deserve respect—and therefore claim not to need it as a form of denial? Or that they are self-respecting enough to not need respect from others? Or that respect from others is not important to them?
Lower need for **interesting conversation** and a **good sense of humor**	It seemed to be "all business" with people who describe themselves as not religious or spiritual. Incidentally, this group also had a significantly lower need for their managers to be cheerful and happy.

In their relationships with others, people who do not consider themselves religious or spiritual have a significantly lower need for shared values, honesty and integrity, trust, unconditional acceptance, loyalty, and a strong work ethic from their managers. They are less likely to need loyalty and respect in their relationships with coworkers, and, compared to people who are religious or spiritual, they don't need managers who are cheerful, happy, compassionate, and fun loving. With this group, life appears to be all business. I would not assume, however, that this group is unhappy, less fulfilled, or otherwise missing something vital in their lives just because they are not religious or spiritual, but the contrast to the religious/spiritual group is profound.

What Managers and Nonmanagers Want from Relationships

In my research on what people want from relationships, I distinguished between respondents who had had managerial experience and those who had not. My reasoning was that people who had been managers would probably have different needs from their relationships with their managers than those who had never been managers, and this turned out to be true. Of the respondents, 72 percent said they had had management roles; 28 percent said they had not.

What Managers Want **(Compared with Nonmanagers)**	
Greater need for **teamwork** and **collaboration** and **cooperation**	Managers had a significantly greater need for teamwork in their relationships with coworkers or peers as well as their own managers, and they had a significantly greater need for collaboration and cooperation from everyone they work with. People in management roles quickly learn not only the value of teamwork but how essential it is to getting work done, so these needs are not surprising.
Greater need for **commitment** and **availability**	Managers were more likely to want the people they work with to be committed to them and to be available when they need them. Most people who have been managers come to appreciate the difficulties of staffing, especially when key people have left the company, so it's natural that they would value people who remain loyal and committed and who are available when staffing needs arise.

Greater need for **encouragement**	These people had a significantly greater need for encouragement from their coworkers or peers. Given the challenges of managerial work, this finding is also not surprising. Managers need to feel that their counterparts in other management positions appreciate the challenges and difficulties of management and are supportive and encouraging.

What Nonmanagers Want (Compared with Managers)

Greater need **to feel competent** and **skilled**	This group consists of individual contributors, experts, technicians, and so on. Not surprisingly, then, they are more likely to need to feel competent and skilled. Their expertise is more than their qualification for the job; it is their source of employment safety. Without it, they may not be employable, at least in their chosen field. And it's important to them that their manager recognizes their competence and skills.
Greater need for **independence**	They have a greater need to be independent, to feel that they answer to no one. Individual contributors often prefer to work in positions in which they are exercising their competence without undue oversight. If you are managing people with a high need for independence, it's important not to micromanage them. That will rankle them more than practically anything else.
Greater need **to be liked**	Nonmanagers have a greater need than managers to feel that others like them, which suggests, on the one hand, that people in nonmanagement roles

Greater need **to be liked** (cont.)	derive much of their job satisfaction from friend-based or more personal relationships than managers do. On the other hand, it suggests that managers have less of a need to be liked because they know that in their role genuine liking from others is an unlikely outcome given the tension inherent in the power differential between them and the people they manage. As much as managers might want to be liked, it often isn't possible when managers have such influence over people's lives. Of course, good managers are often well liked—even loved—by those who report to them (Herb Kelleher at Southwest Airlines comes to mind), but on the whole managers don't derive most of their job satisfaction from being liked.
Greater need *for* **approval**	An interesting corollary is that nonmanagers also have a greater need for approval from close friends and family. It's not clear why this is true. Perhaps a number of people in nonmanagement roles feel that their individual contributor status is a less "successful" role than the roles of people who have been promoted to management positions. By and large, the media do not lionize individual contributors. The popular business press, as well as books and movies about business, generally feature leaders and managers, and people in management positions are often paid more than individual contributors because they have more responsibility. And, of course, managers generally make the decisions that enable the business to grow and prosper (or decline and fail).

As a manager, you can do much to help the individual contributors who work for you get the kind of approval from home that they need. For example, I once worked with an aerospace company team that was writing a massive proposal for a new military airplane. The proposal project was long and arduous, requiring many long days and lost weekends. As the proposal neared completion, the proposal manager sent thank-you cards and flowers to the spouses and significant others of the members on the team. In the cards, he said he appreciated what the families had sacrificed and praised the members of the team for their hard work and dedication. Members of the team later told me that those thank-you cards meant more to their families than just about anything else the company could have done. I think the proposal manager's act was not only great relationship building but also a brilliant example of emotional intelligence.

Notes

Introduction
1. Paul Michelman, "Your New Core Strategy: Employee Retention," *Harvard Business School Working Knowledge* (November 26, 2003), p. 2.

Chapter 3
1. Anne Morrow Lindbergh, *Gift from the Sea* (New York: Pantheon Books, 1955), pp. 23–24.

Chapter 4
1. Pat Wingert and Martha Brant, "Reading Your Baby's Mind," *Newsweek* (August 15, 2005) (http://www.msnbc.msn.com/id/8852928/site/newsweek).
2. Jim Collins, *Good to Great* (New York: HarperCollins, 2001), p. 39.
3. D. Michael Abrashoff, *It's Your Ship: Management Techniques from the Best Damn Ship in the Navy* (New York: Warner Books, 2002).
4. D. Michael Abrashoff interview with Donna Williams (May 4, 2002).

Chapter 6
1. Karen McKibbin, conversation with the author, 2003.
2. In their book *The Leadership Challenge* (San Francisco: Jossey-Bass, 1987), Jim Kouzes and Barry Posner use the expression *encouraging the heart* to talk about recognizing people, celebrating their accomplishments, and demonstrating caring.

Chapter 7

1. James Bandler and Ann Zimmerman, "A Wal-Mart Legend's Trail of Deceit," *Wall Street Journal,* April 8, 2005; Amy Joyce and Carrie Johnson, "Former Wal-Mart Executive to Admit Fraud," *Washington Post,* January 7, 2006. Wal-Mart claims that Bowen participated in the fraud; Bowen is suing the company, saying that he was fired for blowing the whistle on Coughlin.
2. Barbara Kellerman, *Bad Leadership: What It Is, How It Happens, Why It Matters* (Boston: Harvard Business School Press, 2004), p. 135.
3. Malcolm Gladwell, *Blink* (New York: Little, Brown, 2005), p. 14.
4. Robert B. Cialdini, *Influence: The New Psychology of Modern Persuasion* (New York: Quill, 1984), p. 66.

Chapter 8

1. Diane Coutu, "How Resilience Works," *Harvard Business Review* (May 2002).

Appendix

1. The respondents were businesspeople in a variety of industries and companies. Seventy-two percent of them were managers or had had management experience.
2. John Gray, *Men Are from Mars, Women Are from Venus* (New York: Quill, 2004).

Index